Grades K–12

The Portfolio Connection

Student Work Linked to Standards

2nd Edition

Kay Burke

Robin Fogarty

Susan Belgrad

CORWIN PRESS
A SAGE Publications Company
Thousand Oaks, California

D1313923

Copyright © 2002, 1994 by Corwin Press

All rights reserved. When forms and sample documents are included, their use is authorized only by educators, local school sites, and/or noncommercial or nonprofit entities who have purchased the book. Except for that usage, no part of this book may be reproduced or utilized in any form or by any means, electronic or mechanical, including photocopying, recording, or by any information storage and retrieval system, without permission in writing from the publisher.

For information:

Corwin Press
A Sage Publications Company
2455 Teller Road
Thousand Oaks, California 91320
www.corwinpress.com

Sage Publications Ltd.
1 Oliver's Yard
55 City Road
London EC1Y 1SP
United Kingdom

Sage Publications India Pvt. Ltd.
B-42, Panchsheel Enclave
New Delhi 110 017   India

Printed in the United States of America

LCCCN 2001093400
ISBN 1-5751-7439-1

This book is printed on acid-free paper.

05   06   07   08   09   10   9   8   7   6   5   4   3   2   1

The Portfolio Connection

Student Work Linked to Standards

Dedication

In memory of Cindy Stergar who shared her love of teaching and enthusiasm for learning with so many of us.

Contents

Acknowledgments

The Portfolio Connection, envisioned as "just a little book," soon took on the qualities of bread dough rising in 1993 when we began to collaborate on the first edition of this project. It expanded a bit beyond, above, and around the originally designed parameters. The more we wrote, the more we realized the creative potential of portfolios and the excitement generated by their use. This second edition includes additional examples on how portfolios can document students' mastery of the standards. We've also added more criteria checklists and rubrics to focus on how students can self-assess their progress toward meeting their academic goals.

As with any effort of an expansive nature, many hands made the final product possible. First and foremost, we wish to extend a heartfelt thank you to our family members, friends, and colleagues who encouraged us. . . and endured with us. Their support has been unselfish and unending.

We also want to thank those closest to putting all the pieces together editing, designing, and publishing the book. Many thanks to Chris Jaeggi, Sue Schumer, Bruce Leckie, Dave Stockman, Donna Ramirez, and especially to Anne Kaske, our editor whose energy, talents, and skills make our ideas come alive. Portfolios provide a portrait of a student learner over time and evidence of growth and development. In this era of standardized testing, our hopes are that teachers, parents, and policymakers recognize the value of reviewing student work samples, listening to what students say about their work, and reading their reflections about what they have learned.

To all who have worked so hard to make this "little book" possible, we are forever indebted.

Kay, Robin, and Susan
September, 2001

SkyLight Professional Development

Introduction

What Is a Portfolio?

The word *portfolio* connotes many meanings. One might think of an artist collecting his or her best work to present to a studio or client. Another person could envision a stock portfolio containing a person's financial investments. Someone seeking an advertising position would showcase an ability to create compelling ads to a potential employer. Portfolios have been used by architects, photographers, writers, artists, and models over the years to showcase their work. A portfolio is defined as a collection of items organized for a specific purpose and goal.

Portfolios have recently emerged as powerful tools in education. They fall into the category of "performance assessment" where students collect their work samples to show what they have learned. The work samples provide a basis for judging the progress the student is making towards meeting academic goals and standards. It also provides a means to communicate the students' progress to students and parents.

Wortham (2001) says, "Portfolios are a collection of a child's work and teacher data from informal and perform-ance assessments to evaluate development and learning. A portfolio may be kept just by and for the child, with samples of work over a period of time. It may also be organized by the teacher and contain observation reports, checklists, work samples, records of directed assignments, interviews, or other evidence of achievement" (p. 223).

PORTFOLIO:
A collection of items organized for a specific purpose and goal.

Carr and Harris (2001) describe a portfolio as a "purposeful, integrated collection of student work showing effort, progress, or achievement in one or more areas. Usefulness for instruction and assessment is enhanced when students select the items for their portfolios, self-reflection is encouraged, and criteria for success are clear" (p. 181).

Why Use Portfolios?

Portfolios provide information that traditional paper-and-pencil tests cannot. They provide a demonstration of academic skills that helps teachers and students make informal decisions about instruction (Zimmerman 1993). States and school districts currently mandate testing programs to gather data about student achievement. Some states use this data to hold schools, teachers, and students accountable. See Figure 0.1 for reasons that support use of portfolios.

The American Educational Research Association (AERA)

Many people fear there is too much emphasis on test scores and not enough use of multiple measures of assessment. According to a position statement of the American Educational Research Association (AERA) concerning high-stakes testing in PreK–12 education,

Certain uses of achievement test results are termed high stakes if they carry serious consequences for students or for educators. Schools may be judged according to the schoolwide average scores of their students. High schoolwide scores may bring public praise or financial rewards; low scores may bring public embarrassment or heavy sanctions. For individual students, high scores may bring a special diploma attesting to exceptional academic accomplishment; low scores may result in students being held back in grade or denied a high school diploma (Educational Researcher November 2000, p. 24).

PORTFOLIOS:
- offer an alternative assessment to tests
- help achieve a balanced assessment model
- provide a means for informal assessment

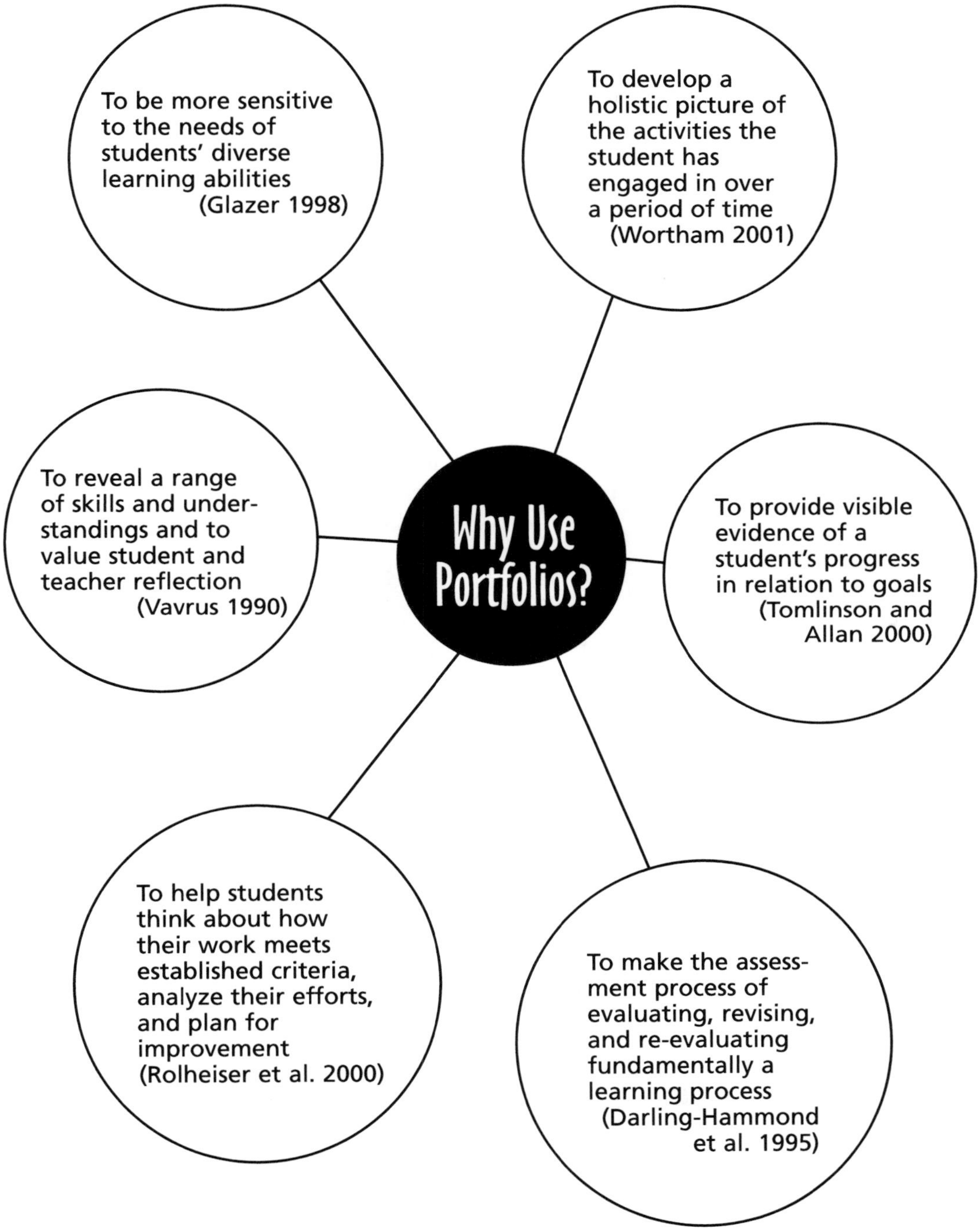

Why Use Portfolios?

To be more sensitive to the needs of students' diverse learning abilities (Glazer 1998)

To develop a holistic picture of the activities the student has engaged in over a period of time (Wortham 2001)

To reveal a range of skills and under-standings and to value student and teacher reflection (Vavrus 1990)

To provide visible evidence of a student's progress in relation to goals (Tomlinson and Allan 2000)

To help students think about how their work meets established criteria, analyze their efforts, and plan for improvement (Rolheiser et al. 2000)

To make the assess-ment process of evaluating, revising, and re-evaluating fundamentally a learning process (Darling-Hammond et al. 1995)

Figure 0.1

AERA is the nation's largest professional organization devoted to the scientific study of education. Their members are concerned about decisions that affect a student's educational—and life—opportunities; they feel such decisions should not be made on the basis of test scores alone. Some of the many issues AERA is concerned about include:

1. adequate resources and opportunities to learn,
2. alignment between the test and the curriculum,
3. validity of passing scores and achievement levels,
4. opportunities for meaningful remediation for examinees who fail high-stakes tests,
5. appropriate attention to language differences among examinees, and
6. appropriate attention to students with disabilities.

(Adapted from AERA, November 2000, pp. 24–25)

AERA members conclude that "when there is credible evidence that a test score may not adequately reflect a student's true proficiency, alternative acceptable means should be provided by which to demonstrate attainment of the tested standards" (AERA, November 2000, p. 24).

Portfolios provide a powerful alternative as well as a complement to standardized tests. They include application of content skills that could offer evidence the student is capable of understanding the information. A portfolio chronicles a student's progress and growth toward meeting curriculum goals and standards. It provides a much richer and more revealing portrait of the student as a learner than the picture captured by a single test score alone.

The Balanced Assessment Model

The Balanced Assessment Model (Fogarty and Stoehr 1995; Burke 2000) advocates using three types of assessment to arrive at an accurate portrait of a student as a learner. The first type of assessment includes traditional tests, quizzes, and standardized tests that focus on assessing the students' knowledge, skills, and mastery of content in the curriculum. Obviously, this type of assessment is necessary and appropriate, but should never be the sole means of determining a student's success, promotion, or graduation or the criteria by which teachers, administrators, and schools are judged. One standardized test score is a single-shot measurement that focuses on verbal/ linguistic and logical/mathematical intelligences. Portfolios, however, chronicle a student's growth and development in their multiple intelligences.

The second type of assessment in the Balanced Assessment Model, the portfolio, focuses on the process the student uses to achieve the goals. Rough drafts and initial problem-solving strategies are dated and attached to final products to show growth over time. Portfolios require students to reflect on their learning, set new goals, and self-evaluate their progress.

The third component of the Balanced Assessment Model focuses on performances—the students' abilities to apply the knowledge, content, and skills they have learned. Performances allow students to demonstrate that they can transfer their knowledge and skills into action. These performances require students to collaborate with peers to create products, projects, or demonstrations according to specific criteria listed in curriculum objectives or learning standards. Students know their performances will be evaluated according to rubrics or scoring guides that provide descriptors for quality work.

> **THE BALANCED ASSESSMENT MODEL:**
> Three types of assessment are used to attain a portrait of the learner: traditional tests, portfolios, and performances.

The percentage of use of each assessment tool depends upon the grade level, the class, and the purpose of the assessment. Teachers need to integrate three types of assessment to meet the individual needs of the students, honor their learning styles, and provide a more accurate evaluation of a student's strengths and weaknesses. The most effective assessment program blends all three types to attain a developmentally appropriate portrait of a student as a learner (see Figure 0.2).

Balanced Assessment

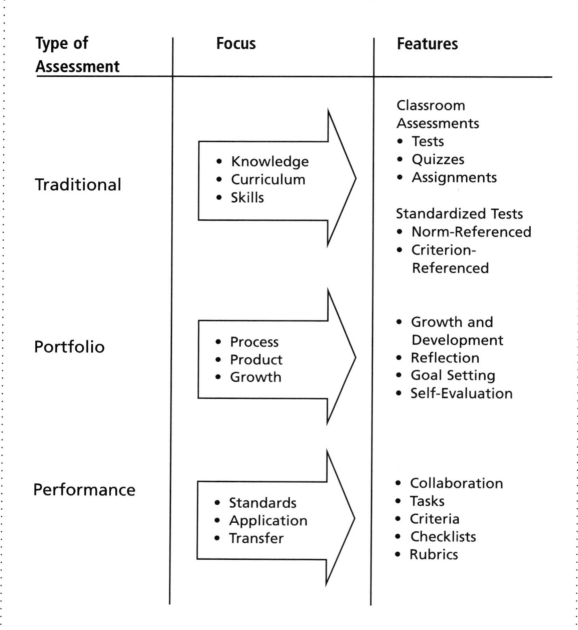

Type of Assessment	Focus	Features
Traditional	• Knowledge • Curriculum • Skills	Classroom Assessments • Tests • Quizzes • Assignments Standardized Tests • Norm-Referenced • Criterion-Referenced
Portfolio	• Process • Product • Growth	• Growth and Development • Reflection • Goal Setting • Self-Evaluation
Performance	• Standards • Application • Transfer	• Collaboration • Tasks • Criteria • Checklists • Rubrics

Adapted from Fogarty and Stoehr, 1995, p. 178.

Figure 0.2 From *How to Assess Authentic Learning,* 3rd Edition, p. xxiv, by K. Burke. © 1999 SkyLight Training and Publishing. Used with permission.

Advantages of Classroom Portfolios

Portfolios help students develop deeper insight into what they are studying. They also allow teachers to assess the students' level of understanding of key concepts because they foster more depth and breadth in the learning process. According to Wiggins and McTighe (1998), going into *depth* on a topic suggests getting below the surface, and *breadth* implies the extensions, variety, and connections needed to relate all the separate ideas. Achieving depth and breadth lead to deeper understanding. It also takes more time.

> Understanding falls through the cracks of testing and grading quite easily. It happens when we pay much attention to knowledge (and thus the easy right–wrong dichotomy in scoring that makes assessment so much easier) and too little attention to the quality of an understanding (clearly a somewhat subjective act). This challenge comes to the fore when we have to justify the grade we have assigned a student to suspicious parents or faraway college admission officers. (Wiggins and McTighe 1998, p. 79)

Gronlund (1998) proposes that portfolios have a number of advantages that make their use worthwhile in the classroom (see Figure 0.3).

Advantages of Using Classroom Portfolios

1. Learning progress over time can be clearly shown (e.g., changes in writing skills).
2. Focusing on students' best work provides a positive influence on learning (e.g., best writing samples).
3. Comparing work to past work fosters greater motivation than comparison to the work of others (e.g., growth in writing skills).
4. Self-assessment skills are increased when students select the best samples of their work and justify their choices (e.g., focus is on criteria of good writing).
5. Portfolios provide for adjustment to individual differences (e.g., students write at their own level but work toward common goals).
6. Portfolios provide for clear communication of learning progress to students, parents, and others (e.g., writing samples obtained at different times can be shown and compared).

From *Assessment of Student Achievement,* 6th edition, p. 158, by N. E. Gronlund. © 1998 Allyn & Bacon. Used with permission.

Figure 0.3

Differentiate Process and Products

Another important advantage of portfolios is that portfolios help teachers differentiate the process and the products students create. Portfolios demonstrate what students have come to know, understand, and be able to do as the result of an extended period of study. Tomlinson and Allan (2000) believe a portfolio of student work is an example of a good product that causes students to "rethink what they have learned, apply what they can do, extend their understanding and skill, and become involved in both critical and creative thinking" (p. 9). Figure 0.4 lists some of the ways to differentiate products or portfolios.

Ways to Differentiate Products

- Allow students to help design products around essential learning goals.

- Encourage students to express what they have learned in varied ways.

- Allow for varied working arrangements (for example, working alone or as part of a team to complete the product).

- Provide or encourage the use of varied types of resources in preparing products.

- Provide product assignments at varying degrees of difficulty to match student readiness.

- Use a wide variety of kinds of assessments.

- Work with students to develop rubrics of quality that allow for demonstration of both whole-class and individual goals.

Figure 0.4 From *Leadership for Differentiating Schools & Classrooms* by C. A. Tomlinson and S. D. Allan. © 2000 Association for Supervision and Curriculum Development. Reprinted by permission. All rights reserved.

Support Individual Learning

Portfolio use also dovetails with research about how students learn best. Beamon (2001) discusses how adolescents' views of school vary according to random biological and environmental factors that have affected how they feel about themselves. She says that "though all are capable of learning, some respond uniformly to one style of teaching, one curriculum, one mode of assessment, one cultural perspective, or necessarily, one learning" (p. 3). The learning of adolescents is enhanced when individual differences are acknowledged. Figure 0.5 addresses some conditions that support their learning.

Conditions That Support Adolescent Learning

Adolescents learn better when they . . .

- encounter learning that is appropriate to their developmental level and is presented in multiple ways and in an enjoyable and interesting manner.

- are intellectually intrigued by tasks that are "authentic" and perceived as challenging, novel, and relevant to their own lives.

- are allowed to share and discuss ideas, and to work together on tasks, projects, and problems.

- are afforded multiple strategies to acquire, integrate, and interpret knowledge meaningfully, to demonstrate understanding, and to apply knowledge to new situations.

- are provided opportunities to develop and use strategic thinking skills, such as reasoning and problem solving.

- are given guidance and feedback about their work, yet are permitted to monitor personal progress and understanding.

- are in a safe, supportive environment where value is given to personal ideas and negative emotions (such as fear of punishment and embarrassment) are minimized.

From *Teaching with Adolescent Learning in Mind,* p. 6, by G. Beamon. ©2000 SkyLight Training and Publishing. Used with permission.

Figure 0.5

Portfolios afford students multiple strategies to construct meaning from information and experiences and to demonstrate their mastery of standards. Teachers have a viable method to differentiate learning and assessment to meet the diverse needs of their students.

Authentic Learning and Assessment

One of the keys to a successful portfolio system includes using a variety of assessments. The portfolio would be no different than a work folder if it included only tests, quizzes, work sheets, and homework assignments. Authentic assessments focus on students' ability to produce quality products and performances. Authentic assessments derive from authentic intellectual work. Newmann, Bryk, and Nagaoka (2001) state that authentic intellectual work involves

> original application of knowledge and skills, rather than just routine use of facts and procedures. It also entails disciplined inquiry into the details of a particular problem and results in a product or presentation that has meaning or value beyond success in school. We summarize these distinctive characteristics of authentic intellectual work as construction of knowledge, through the use of disciplined inquiry, to produce discourse, products, or performances that have value beyond school (p. 10).

Authentic assessments provide the context for portfolio development because they highlight the criteria for what should be included (see Figure 0.6).

Repertoire of Assessments

The portfolio provides a fully realized portrait of the student as a learner because it utilizes a rich palette of assessment tools. A standardized test or teacher-made test emphasizes verbal/linguistic and logical/mathematical skills. A portfolio showcases a student's multiple intelligences by including artifacts that also tap his visual/spatial, musical/rhythmic, interpersonal, intrapersonal, bodily/kinesthetic, and naturalist intelligences. The portfolio reflects assessment tools that allow students multiple mediums and multiple opportunities to showcase their learnings (see Figure 0.7).

Digital Connection

Portfolios lend themselves to technology—digital portfolios solve storage issues, ease data retrieval and file management, and improve the portfolio process.

Criteria for Authentic Assessments

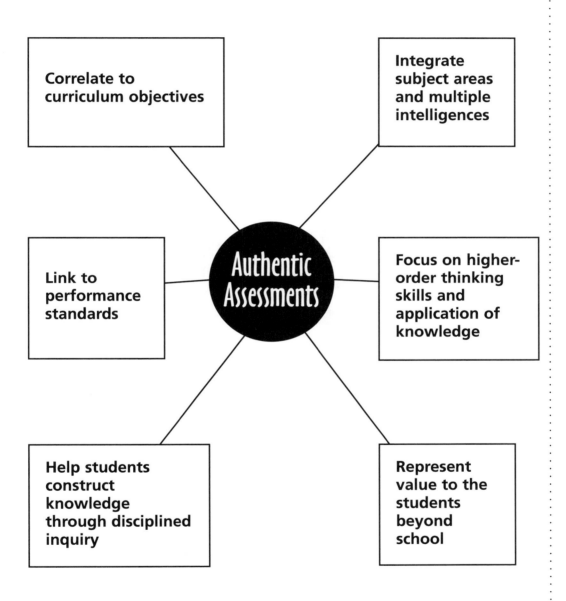

Figure 0.6

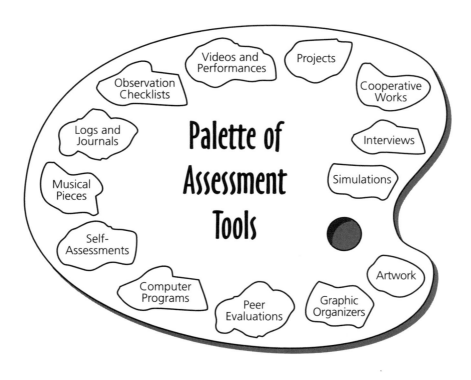

Figure 0.7

Self-Assessment—The Power of Reflection

The real power of the portfolio emerges when students describe the work they include, discuss the key concepts they have learned, and most importantly, reflect on how this learning has affected them. A portfolio is really a multisensory and multidimensional personification of a student's learning. As Gronlund (1998) warns, "Simply collecting samples of student work and putting it in a file does not provide for effective use of the portfolio" (p. 158). If students merely collect and store work in a folder, they minimize the effectiveness of using the work as an effective instructional and assessment tool.

Adding the critical element of reflection fosters the higher-order critical thinking and decision-making skills necessary for continuous learning and improvement. According to Rolheiser, Bower, and Stevahn (2000), "Reflection happens when students think about how their work meets established criteria; they analyze the effectiveness of their efforts, and plan for improvement. Reflecting on what has been learned and articulating that learning to others is the heart and soul of the portfolio process. Without reflection, a portfolio has little meaning" (p. 31).

Reflection is the heart and soul of the portfolio process because it enhances the learner's ability to self-assess her work and analyze her strengths and weaknesses in order to set new goals for growth. The metacognitive process of "thinking about one's thinking" is critical to the success of a portfolio. The student takes control of her own learning by becoming an informed critic of her own work. The teacher and parents serve as "guides on the side," but the student builds the capacity to self-assess, redirect, and refine her own work.

Costa and Kallick (1992) warn, "We must constantly remind ourselves that the ultimate purpose of evaluation is to have students become self-evaluating. If students graduate from our schools still dependent upon others to tell them when they are adequate, good, or excellent, then we have missed the whole point of what education is about" (p. 280).

> **REFLECTION:**
> - enhances self-assessment
> - analyzes strengths and weaknesses
> - sets goals for growth

The Portfolio Process

The richness of the portfolio as a valuable assessment tool may be evident to educators, but the reality is that implementing an effective portfolio system is very time consuming. The collection of student work, the selection of key items, and periodic reviews to evaluate student progress require considerable time and effort by students and teachers (Gronlund 1998). Several questions are raised by educators:

- Where do I start?
- Where will I store everything?
- Who determines what goes in the portfolio?
- How will I grade it?
- Do I keep it for a whole year?

These are just some of the nitty-gritty organizational questions that must be answered before embarking on a portfolio journey. There are no right answers to these questions—each situation is different. This book explores ideas to consider in order to create a workable portfolio system that provides an accurate accountability system for the teacher that also meets the individual needs of the students. An outline appears below; a brief summary of each section follows.

Chapter 1   Project Academic Purposes
Chapter 2   Interject Standards and Criteria
Chapter 3   Connect to Curriculum Goals
Chapter 4   Collect and Organize
Chapter 5   Select Key Artifacts
Chapter 6   Inspect to Self-Assess
Chapter 7   Reflect Metacognitively
Chapter 8   Perfect and Evaluate
Chapter 9   Respect and Celebrate Accomplishments

Chapter 1— Project Academic Purposes

Early in the process, educators address the purpose for using portfolios. Purposes include self-assessment and reflection, assessment and evaluation, meeting curriculum goals and standards, or reporting progress. Often, portfolios combine many purposes, but the purpose must be established in order to focus on the process to achieve the goal.

Chapter 2— Interject Standards and Criteria

Standards-based portfolios provide evidence of teacher and student accountability. When assignments are correlated to district or state content and performance standards, teachers and students submit documentation that the standards have been addressed and evidence of students' progress toward meeting or exceeding the standards.

The standard can appear on each piece of work or separate folders or sections can be used to designate specific standards. The entries filed within them can demonstrate not only completion, but also quality.

Chapter 3—Connect to Curriculum Goals

Teachers are responsible for covering the content and processes in their curriculum. Sometimes the curriculum uses a scope and sequence organization; other times it lists the content pieces to be addressed in each grade level or course. The curriculum drives instruction and students' understanding of content must be included in the portfolio. Knowledge of content could also be the purpose of the portfolio. Using content to demonstrate processes such as writing, speaking, and problem solving could be another purpose. In most cases, teachers integrate content and process to provide evidence of knowledge and application of knowledge.

Chapter 4—Collect and Organize

Often teachers have students collect everything they do in class and save it in a "working portfolio." Sometimes teachers do not know the requirements in advance, so they ask students to save everything until it is time to organize the artifacts by standard, curriculum goal, topic, or subject area. The working portfolio could be a hanging file, notebook, cereal box, or any large container that can store papers, projects, cassettes, and videotapes.

Portfolios can help teachers integrate content and process to provide evidence of knowledge and application of knowledge.

Chapter 5—Select Key Artifacts

Criteria determine what pieces should be selected from the working portfolio to go in the final portfolio. Pieces in the final portfolio show how the student meets the predetermined goal. The final portfolio includes only the items that provide evidence of meeting the goals—not everything the student has completed. The "less is more" philosophy guides this phase of portfolio development.

Chapter 6—Inspect to Self-Assess

Since many of the portfolio entries include projects, products, and performances, traditional multiple-choice tests are not valid methods of evaluating the work. Criteria checklists provide specific indicators students need to master in order to perform appropriately on each assignment. The students can assess their own work as well as assist peers in determining if they meet the criteria. Teachers use checklists to monitor student work and provide assistance throughout the process. The ongoing or formative feedback during the inspection stage improves the quality of student work.

Chapter 7—Reflect Metacognitively

Since reflection is the heart and soul of portfolios, students should always write reflections about what they have learned, how they have learned it, and what insight they have gained about their learning and themselves. The descriptions of their work help teachers and parents get a better understanding of whether or not they have grasped the important concepts of the learning. More importantly, the reflections reveal how the student has internalized the learning and connected it to his or her own life.

Chapter 8—Perfect and Evaluate

Even though the students may have done their very best work, they still need to examine how well they did meeting the goals and standards. "Trying real hard" may show effort and positive attitude, but parents and the public in general still need to know if students met curriculum goals and the standards. Rubrics provide specific guidelines and levels of quality that help students self-evaluate their work. They also help teachers grade the student fairly and consistently according to known standards of quality work. Most importantly, the evaluation of student work helps the teacher select different teaching strategies to help the students improve.

Chapter 9—Respect and Celebrate Accomplishments

The portfolio conference helps teachers, parents, and students talk about learning. The conversations related to work provide valuable insights into the students' understanding as well as open discussions about alternative strategies to meet academic goals. Portfolio exhibitions celebrate learning by allowing people other than the teacher to share the students' learning by showcasing their growth and progress. Students have a purpose for doing well and many welcome sharing their work with a larger audience.

Figure 0.8 summarizes the portfolio process.

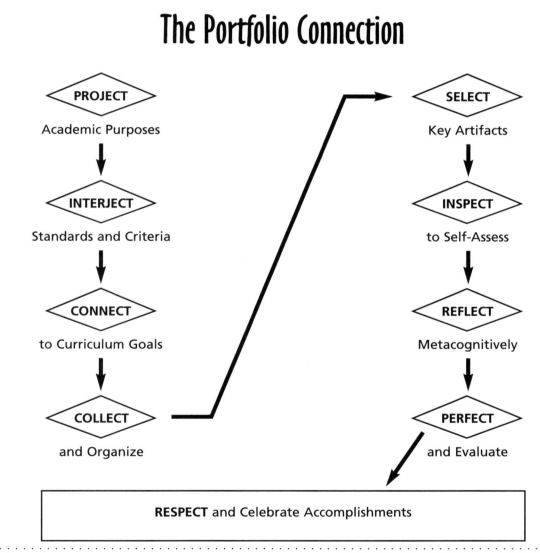

The Portfolio Connection

PROJECT
Academic Purposes

INTERJECT
Standards and Criteria

CONNECT
to Curriculum Goals

COLLECT
and Organize

SELECT
Key Artifacts

INSPECT
to Self-Assess

REFLECT
Metacognitively

PERFECT
and Evaluate

RESPECT and Celebrate Accomplishments

Figure 0.8

Each chapter includes an Examples page and Blackline masters. The Examples show how teachers incorporate portfolio ideas and methods into their classrooms. Teachers may photocopy and use the Blackline masters to plan or implement the portfolio process in their classrooms. A Sample Portfolio appears in the Appendix.

The Journey

The portfolio provides a framework that allows students to showcase their originality within the context of a meaningful assessment tool.

What would motivate teachers to undertake a portfolio system when they are already overwhelmed by mandates to increase test scores, cover objectives in four-inch thick curriculum guides, and manage the behavior of culturally, academically, physically, and socially diverse students? The thrill of victory? The desire for greatness? The love of a challenge? The search for something to fill class time? Even though portfolios present many organizational and time-management challenges, most teachers instinctively feel they are worth the effort. Teachers, like many parents and students, recognize that standardized tests used as a single measure of student achievement are not accurate representations of many students' capabilities.

Teachers are searching for ways to meet the needs of students of diverse cultures and values, diverse learning abilities, and diverse learning styles. Glazer (1998) says that many assessment procedures have been insensitive to the diversities in classrooms as a result of people's misunderstanding of assessment and evaluation. She warns that "for most, tests, testing, and the resulting test scores prevail as indicators of achievement" (p. 20). Glazer also feels that by electing appropriate assessment tools and instructional strategies, teachers can respect the originality each student brings to a classroom. The portfolio provides a framework that allows students to showcase their originality within the context of a meaningful assessment tool.

Instruction is assessment and assessment is instruction. As Paulson, Paulson, and Meyer (1991) state: "[Portfolios] can be powerful educational tools for encouraging students to take charge of their learning. . . . If carefully assembled, portfolios become an intersection of instruction and assessment; they are not just instruction or just assessment, but, rather, both. Together, instruction and assessment give more than either give separately" (p. 61).

Project Academic Purposes

Overview

Portfolios are among the most frequently mentioned alternatives in the current repertoire of authentic assessment tools. Portfolios, however, are used in many different ways and their purposes and structure are still being defined. Once educators establish the primary purposes for using portfolios to assess learning, the implementation process evolves.

Before introducing portfolios as assessment tools, it is critical that teachers look at the "big picture" to determine the primary and secondary uses of portfolios.

Teachers need to ask the hard questions:

- How will students be involved in the ongoing process of gathering artifacts?
- How are portfolios going to be used?
- What is the real purpose of this tool?
- How will portfolios be organized?
- How will portfolios reflect student growth?
- How can portfolios provide concrete evidence students meet or exceed the standards?

> **PORTFOLIO PURPOSE:**
>
> Before the portfolio process begins, the portfolio's primary and secondary uses must be determined. The _purpose_ of the portfolio is the same as _how_ the portfolio will be used. The portfolio's purpose will inform the choice of portfolio type.

The last question is perhaps the most important. The purposes for the portfolio are determined by the objectives the teacher has for the assessment. Wortham (2001) states, "If the purpose is to assess development for a reporting period, an evaluative portfolio with a development format will be chosen" (p. 229). She also explains that if the purpose for portfolios is only for parent conferences, then a showcase portfolio might be chosen. Portfolios can be excellent tools for both students and teachers once the principal players discuss and agree on the rationale. After the big picture is in place, the process of implementing an effective portfolio system begins. (See Blackline 1.1 at the end of this chapter for a blackline master to use when planning for portfolio purpose and types.)

Introduction

Portfolios have the potential to reveal a lot about their creators. They can become a window into the students' heads, a
means for both staff and students to understand the educational process at the level of the individual learner. They can
be powerful educational tools for encouraging students to
take charge of their own learning. . . .

(Paulson et al. 1991, p. 61).

Portfolios come in all shapes and sizes. Many students produce
electronic portfolios that integrate authentic learning, assessment of
standards, and technology to provide a more complete portrait of
themselves as learners (Ash 2000). A portfolio is more than a final

Portfolios: A Window into the Student's Head

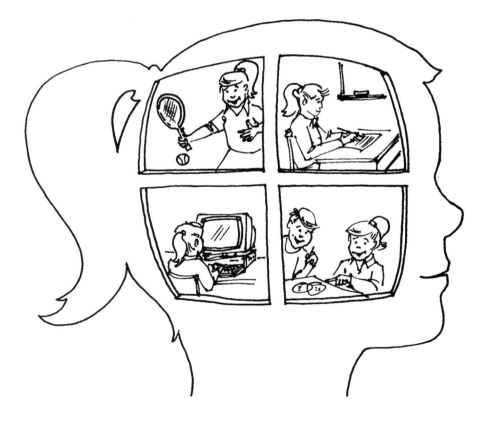

Digital Connection

Digital portfolios use the
power of computers as
telecommunication tools to
showcase students' achievements. The joining of computer technology applications
with the communication power
of the Internet has brought
the digital (i.e., electronic)
portfolio into the teaching
and learning repertoire of
today's educators.

product students turn in to fulfill their course requirements. A portfolio is also a process that enables students to become active and thoughtful learners. The process of collecting and selecting items to include in the portfolio helps students reflect on their own learning and achieve deeper understanding.

Purposes of Portfolios

The purpose of a portfolio guides the process of creating it. Teachers need to determine why they are going to use portfolios with students before they implement a portfolio system. Oftentimes, one portfolio achieves several purposes.

Meet Standards

When the purpose of the portfolio is to show evidence that the students are making progress towards meeting district or state standards, the teacher requires a portfolio that includes each standard in the subject or grade level. Students add work in each section to provide documentation that the standard was met or is "in progress." Often, the teacher dictates specific assignments, such as a persuasive essay or a mathematics problem. But just including a specific assignment in the portfolio is not enough. A checklist or scoring guide should be attached to each item to describe the quality of the student's work. The standards portfolio used in conjunction with student grades and authentic performances provides a more balanced assessment of each students' strengths and weaknesses and a clearer portrait of the student as a learner.

Show Growth and Development

Since a portfolio showcases students' work over time, dated entries provide a portrait of a "learner in motion." Students, parents, and teachers monitor academic and social growth throughout the year. A paragraph written in September may include many errors and lack focus, but a paragraph written in December shows improvement in both areas. Teachers document where a student is at the beginning of

Digital Connection

Digital portfolios have great potential for showcasing students' achievement of standards. The digital portfolio broadly communicates the outcomes of teaching and learning at all levels of schooling—elementary, middle, secondary, and post-secondary. Potential audiences who view the standards-based portfolio go beyond peers, teachers, parents, school staff, and administrators to include the local community and beyond.

the year or at the point the student enters the class, and then tracks the student's progress throughout the year. Portfolios become running records of students' progress over time and help them recognize their own strengths and weaknesses.

Portfolios accommodate students' diversity by providing baseline data of each student's skill sets and knowledge base. They also allow students to demonstrate their learning through a wide variety of multiple intelligences and authentic learning situations. Since most classes today are heterogeneously grouped, the work in portfolios documents the entry point of each student. This documentation supplies the baseline data that is necessary to measure growth.

PURPOSES OF PORTFOLIOS:
- To meet standards
- To show growth and development
- To demonstrate content and process knowledge
- To help students self-assess
- To integrate learning

Demonstrate Content and Process Knowledge

The portfolio demonstrates a student's knowledge and understanding of a content area. Artifacts showcase knowledge of mathematics, science, art, music, or industrial arts. The items contained in the portfolio indicate not only the knowledge, but also the application of that knowledge through papers, products, performances, and projects. These artifacts demonstrate the students' content knowledge and their ability to apply that knowledge using lifelong learning skills such as writing, reading, problem solving, and decision making.

Can we just guess or do you want us to explain our answers?

Help Students Self-Assess

Wolf (1989) asserts that one purpose of the portfolio is to have students learn to assess their own progress as learners. When students review and reflect on their work, they engage in a self-assessment process that fosters lifelong learning. The primary purpose of this type of portfolio is metacognitive reflection—the student monitors and celebrates his or her own growth and development. When a student leaves the classroom or school, that student alone is responsible for directing his learning. The teacher with a red pen is no longer available to provide the feedback to direct or redirect the student. Students who are able to critically evaluate their own work become more independent and self-confident learners.

Integrate Learning

Fogarty and Stoehr (1995) believe that students need to make connections between topics and among subject areas (see Figure 1.1). The integrated portfolio contains assignments and artifacts from different subject areas. For example, middle school and junior high students study themes or concepts that link across content areas. Students recognize the relationships among different content areas and understand how important it is to integrate learning to achieve a goal. The theme of change, for example, connects across literature, science, social studies. Students relate to the commonalties of the concept as it relates to different subject areas.

Types of Portfolios

Once teachers determine the central purpose or combination of purposes for implementing a portfolio system, they then consider the type of portfolio that can best achieve these purposes. The following types used by themselves or in combination with other ideas fulfill the purposes of the portfolio. These types can be classified into three categories: personal, academic, or professional.

Digital Connection

When deciding whether or not to use digital portfolios, teachers, parents, administrators, and district decision makers must jointly study their anticipated impact and develop policies that promote student learning while protecting student confidentiality and individuality.

Personal Portfolios

Scrapbook Portfolio

Items from outside of school included in this portfolio form a more holistic picture of the students. The entire portfolio focuses on students' hobbies, community activities, musical or artistic talents, sports, families, pets, or travels. Artifacts include pictures, awards, videos, and memorabilia. Students can also include a written or videotaped autobiographical sketch, career or college goals, future travel or family plans, and reflections on what they need to accomplish to make their dreams or career plans a reality. This portfolio helps classmates and teachers get to know students and celebrates their interests and successes outside the traditional confines of school.

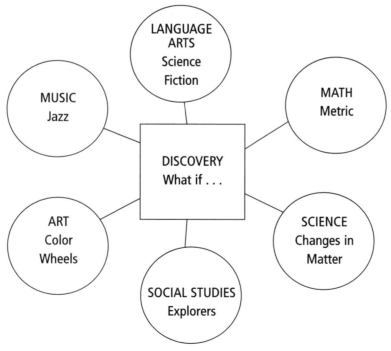

Integrated Portfolio

Adapted from *Integrating the Curricula with Multiple Intelligences: Teams, Themes, and Threads,* p. 93, by R. Fogarty and J. Stoehr. © 1995 IRI/SkyLight Training and Publishing. Used with permission.

Figure 1.1

Best Work Portfolio

The best work portfolio, popular at the elementary school level, includes items that may or may not have been graded previously. This type of portfolio allows students to select entries from all the work they have done. Student choice forms an important component. Once the teacher and the students select key items, they review the work and discover students' growth and development in areas that may not be assessed on teacher-made tests or on standardized tests. This type of portfolio highlights the strengths of the students and helps bolster their sense of self-esteem and self-worth.

Content Portfolio

Educators teaching a single subject area such as mathematics, science, language arts, art, music, and industrial arts require students to demonstrate their knowledge of that content area. For example, language arts teachers may ask students to include one example of each of the following in their content portfolios: narrative essay, expository essay, persuasive essay, response to literature, poem, letter, research paper, and book report. The teacher may require that one persuasive essay be included in the portfolio, but the student chooses which persuasive essay to include.

> **STANDARDS PORTFOLIO:**
> Items provide evidence of students meeting or exceeding the standards. Checklists, scoring guides, or rubrics are attached and indicate the quality of the work.

Academic Portfolios

Standards Portfolio

Teachers assign work that demonstrates the students have met specific standards. The portfolio is divided into standards such as:

1. Students will read with understanding and fluency.
2. Students will write to communicate for a variety of purposes.
3. Students listen and speak effectively in a variety of situations.

Students include items that provide evidence that they have met or exceeded the standards. The pieces usually have a checklist or scoring guide, also known as a rubric, attached to indicate the quality of students' work and the areas in which to improve in order to meet the standards. The standards portfolio is becoming more popular as a means of documenting academic achievement and ensuring teacher accountability. (For a blackline master to help in planning a standards portfolio, use Blackline 1.2 at the end of the chapter.)

Integrated Portfolio

The integrated portfolio encourages students, teachers, and parents to view the whole student by seeing a body of work from all the disciplines and to show connections between or among the subjects included (Cole et al. 2000). Students select items from several or all of their subjects. They discuss the concepts or skills that cross several subject areas and connect with ideas outside of school. The integrated portfolio works well in elementary schools where teachers work on topic units, such as spiders. Students include readings, mathematics problems, science projects, artworks, and music pieces all related to spiders. Integrated portfolios for junior high or middle schools work best when a team of teachers plan the curriculum together. The team selects a theme, such as conflict or justice in America. Students include responses to literature from English, statistics from mathematics, issues of experimentation from science, and art and music projects related to the theme. The integrated portfolio helps students see the connections among all the disciplines and provides a more holistic or integrated learning experience. (For a blackline master to help in planning an integrated portfolio, see Blackline 1.3 at the end of this chapter.)

Cooperative Group Portfolio

Each member of the cooperative group contributes items that showcase individual strengths. Group items—samples or pictures of group projects, performances, team-building activities, and school or community projects—demonstrate the power of the cooperative group. Criteria determined by the students guide them in their self-assessments. Group portfolios may be used for conferences with other groups, teachers, and parents. A group portfolio emphasizes various strengths and talents students bring to the group and fosters collaborative relationships.

Multiyear Portfolio

Some schools cluster grade levels together in two-, three-, or four-year intervals and require students to save specific portfolio pieces from each year. For example, students save items from kindergarten, first, and second grade in different colored folders. The folder for each grade level can be placed in an accordion folder and stored at the school. Periodically, students get out their work, reflect on their progress, and note their improvements. Students review their artwork, scientific inquiries, problem-solving activities, handwriting, cassette recordings of themselves reading, etc. They also ask their peers to review their work and offer feedback. These multiyear portfolios also chronicle students' progress toward mastering standards. Since students develop skills and abilities at different times, teachers track their progress and differentiate the curriculum to meet the individual learning needs of each student. (For a blackline master to use with students who are creating multiyear portfolios, see Blackline 1.4 at the end of this chapter.)

MULTIPLE INTELLIGENCES:
- visual/spatial
- logical/mathematical
- verbal/linguistic
- musical/rhythmic
- interpersonal
- intrapersonal
- bodily/kinesthetic
- naturalist

Multiple Intelligences Portfolio

Schools seeking to ensure the success of students with diverse needs and learning styles implement the multiple intelligences portfolio to showcase all aspects of the students' talents. The portfolios include activities and assessments based on Gardner's (1983, 1993) multiple intelligences: visual/spatial, logical/mathematical, verbal/linguistic, musical/rhythmic, interpersonal, intrapersonal, bodily/kinesthetic, and naturalist. Students empowered to make choices include a variety of entries such as visuals, cassette recordings, videotapes, and pictures to showcase their abilities and their personalities.

Class Profile Portfolio

For this type of portfolio, each class compiles items to chronicle its accomplishments and to provide a portrait of the class. Items may include:

- class picture, motto, or song;
- class predictions;
- last wills and testaments for the next class;
- pictures or videos of class or community projects, performances, field trips, assemblies, or guest speakers; and
- letters from parents, administrators, congressional representatives, business leaders, or sports or movie personalities.

The class portfolio can include group projects or examples of team-building activities that helped bond the class together. To provide a comprehensive portrait, include class poems, stories, biographical information, profiles, computer programs, accomplishments, short- or long-term goals, career choices, or a collage of famous people in the news or of students in the class.

Intelligent Behaviors Portfolios

Teachers promoting intelligent and socially responsible behaviors for their students develop portfolios to focus on these behaviors. Intelligent behaviors include evidence of persistence, empathic listening, flexibility in thinking, metacognitive awareness, problem posing, and problem solving (Costa 1991). These behaviors transcend content areas and highlight dispositions that transfer into life and help students become successful and thoughtful adults.

Schoolwide Profile Portfolio

For this portfolio the principal compiles a schoolwide portfolio to chronicle the school year. Entries in the portfolio include schoolwide events such as campus beautification day, field day, school olympics, or international day. Other entries include:

- pictures or videos of sporting events,
- special speakers at assemblies,
- schoolwide awards,
- field trips,
- lists of students on honor rolls,
- autographed playbills from school plays,
- party invitations and photos, and
- information from PTA/PTO nights.

Digital Connection

Since the introduction of presentation software such as *Hypercard* and *Powerpoint*, it has become clear that technology can bring the life and achievements of classrooms into the wider school community. With proper attention to policy and procedures, the digital class portfolio provides a way for students to demonstrate and celebrate their unique accomplishments.

In addition, the portfolio can showcase National Merit Scholarship winners, student or teacher awards, science fair projects, or musical performances. Students, teachers, parents, or administrators contribute the descriptions and reflections. The school portfolio is kept in the school office or media center or on the school Web site for the public to review (Bernhardt 1994) and could be used as a document in a schoolwide review, strategic plan, or accreditation study.

> **PORTFOLIO:**
> Adds dimension to the student profile beyond information captured by grades and standardized test scores.

Time Capsule Portfolio

For a time capsule portfolio, students select key items, write predictions for the future, and bury the artifacts in a time capsule to be dug up in five or ten years. Once a cycle is started, schools can bury a time capsule and dig one up each year to symbolize the connections among classes. The time capsule portfolio documents the history of a school for future generations and provides a sense of community and historical perspective.

Districtwide Profile Portfolio

Districts may keep a cumulative portfolio that includes contributions from each of the schools as well as districtwide events. Some events to include in a districtwide portfolio are

- science or book fairs,
- community projects,
- scores on standardized tests,
- scholarship winners,
- schools of excellence,
- physical fitness awards,
- state or federal grants,
- computer innovations, and
- awards that students, teachers, and administrators earn.

The districtwide portfolio provides documentation to show how the district meets accreditation requirements or standards. This type of portfolio reveals the district's strengths and weaknesses and is instrumental in planning future instructional goals. The portfolios contain analyses of test scores, absentee rates, graduation rates, and progress toward meeting school improvement goals. Often this portfolio is shared with the parents or the school board periodically to help guide strategic planning efforts.

Professional Portfolios

College Admissions Portfolio

Since university officials are beginning to criticize the use of high-stakes aptitude tests like the Scholastic Assessment Test (SAT) as the key predictor of future academic success, they are exploring alternate criteria to consider for admissions. Some colleges and universities require prospective freshmen to prepare portfolios that contain samples of their high school work. The college admissions and placement personnel review evidence of the student's abilities in all subject areas as well as extracurricular and community activities to determine the student's potential contribution to their college. Colleges review the portfolio as part of the acceptance process. Many admissions officers feel the portfolio adds a richer dimension to the student profile when used in conjunction with grade point averages and standardized test scores. Some colleges do not require a portfolio for the acceptance process, but they do use the portfolio for placement in academic courses once the student has been accepted.

College Scholarship Portfolio

Portfolios containing academic transcripts, attendance and discipline records, standardized test scores, and other pertinent information can be submitted when students apply for academic or athletic scholarships. Scholarship portfolios also include letters of recommendation, commendations, videos, news stories, programs, yearbooks, playbills, and any other information that illustrates why the student should be awarded financial assistance. The portfolio provides a more complete portrait of the student as a well-rounded individual by showcasing performances that are not always reflected in grades or test scores but could qualify the student for scholarship consideration or financial aid.

Digital Connection

With the ease of use of Web-editing software, more students today are able to design Web pages that include the items needed to apply for college scholarships. This digital portfolio is rapidly finding an important place in the college admissions and financial assistance arena.

Employability Portfolio

Some schools, school districts, and states require students to collect evidence of their employability skills. Students are asked to show their academic work as well as evidence of their ability to communicate, to work in a group, and to work responsibly. Students are sometimes asked to compile a portfolio for a mock job search. They practice interview techniques and appropriate behavior during an interview. During the mock interview, the students discuss the contents of their portfolios and summarize why they should be hired. Members of the business community volunteer to conduct these mock interviews and critique the students' performances. "Hiring" decisions are based on the portfolio, résumé, oral presentation, and interview. Since many employers are beginning to ask for portfolios, students who understand the process will be better prepared to utilize portfolios effectively in their job searches. (For a form to help students choose items for an employability portfolio, see Blackline 1.5 at the end of this chapter.)

Preservice Portfolio—Intern Returns

More and more undergraduate education programs require preservice teachers to keep a portfolio of entries that demonstrate their mastery of curriculum goals and course standards. The portfolio could contain any or all of the following:

- lists of courses taken,
- sample lesson plans,
- reading lists,
- artifacts of students' work,
- samples of extracurricular activities,
- videotapes or cassettes of lessons taught in the classroom,
- interviews with students,
- summaries of workshops or seminars attended,
- evidence of peer coaching,
- copies of evaluations,
- letters from students and parents,
- long-term goals, and
- self-evaluations of the teaching experience.

Student teachers often keep ongoing logs and journals of their teaching experiences along with personal reflections and feedback from supervising teachers, mentors, or college supervisors.

Some colleges of education also require students to submit a portfolio that meets the standards developed by Interstate New Teacher Assessment and Support Consortium (INTASC) (McLaughlin and Vogt 1996). The education majors demonstrate their knowledge of subject area, ability to meet students' instructional needs, interactive instructional techniques, classroom management strategies, assessment plans, and professionalism (Campbell et al. 1997).

The portfolio is not only a graduation requirement—it can also be used in the interview process when applying for a teaching position. Prospective employers interested in teacher performance ask applicants to bring a teaching portfolio to initial interviews. Principals and directors of personnel can determine if the potential employees have experiences in the innovative educational strategies they value. If the district incorporates cooperative learning, positive discipline, multiple intelligences, or authentic assessment in classes, they prefer to hire teachers who already understand and practice these concepts rather than invest in additional staff development training. A portfolio interview gives insight into a prospective teacher's teaching preparation.

Teacher Portfolio—Teacher as Researcher

Teachers model how to use portfolios by compiling their own professional portfolios. The portfolio documents achievement of short- and long-term goals. For example, a group of teachers may have a pre-conference with their supervisor and list cooperative learning as their goal for the next school year. The teachers engage in an action research project to collect data (Schmuck 1997). The portfolio contains pictures, videos, lesson plans, and artifacts that validate the teachers' implementation of cooperative learning in classrooms. The artifacts are reviewed in the post-conference to determine if the teachers fulfilled the stated goal to implement cooperative learning (Burke 1997).

Digital Connection

Teachers and administrators also serve as models of the applications of technology and telecommunication as they design and share their own portfolios of action research or professional inquiry.

Digital portfolios provide the opportunity and context for shared inquiry, reflection, and accomplished teaching. The by-product is the transfer of the processes of creating a digital professional portfolio into elementary, middle, and secondary classrooms.

Administrator Portfolio—The Principal's Principles

Administrators compile evidence to showcase leadership abilities and document their progress in meeting strategic goals. Their portfolios may include:

- schoolwide planning models,
- mission statements,
- examples of strategic or site-based planning meetings,
- innovative programs,
- commendations,
- integrated units,
- schoolwide test scores,
- financial records, and
- documentation of professional improvement (courses, seminars, inservices) attended by the administrator or provided by the administrator for the staff. (Dietz 2001)

School boards, superintendents, and prospective employers may want evidence that the administrator has knowledge or experience in a variety of areas. Those areas include:

- inclusion,
- differentiated learning,
- cooperative learning,
- site-based management,
- total quality schools,
- higher-order thinking strategies,
- problem-based learning,
- integrated curricula,
- multiple intelligences,
- authentic assessment,
- consensus building,
- nongraded schools, and
- topics related to school reform that correlate to the district's goals.

Since the school leader sets the tone for the whole school, district personnel want to see evidence of an administrator's knowledge of the best educational practices and commitment to the teachers and students. Administrators also compile evidence for a school leader's portfolio that includes artifacts to meet the Interstate School Leaders Licensure Consortium (ISLLC) standards (Brown and Irby 1997). See the sidebar on the right for a list of ISLLC standards. Many administrators are evaluated by the evidence they provide to show they have met each of the standards.

Teacher Evaluation Portfolio—Performance Reviews

The traditional system of teacher evaluation is evolving. Teachers today may be asked to provide a portfolio to show they have met state professional standards or met a goal-related standard linked to improved student achievement. Burke (1997) describes a goal-setting portfolio where teachers implement new teaching strategies and collect data to meet their goals.

ISLLC STANDARDS:
- Vision of Learning
- School Culture
- Learning Environment
- Collaboration
- Ethics
- Political, Social, and Cultural Contexts

Danielson (1996) describes four domains of professional portfolios:

1. planning and preparation;
2. the classroom environment;
3. instruction; and
4. professional responsibilities.

Teachers include artifacts in their portfolios from each domain as part of their performance reviews. These portfolios can also be digital portfolios that include video pieces of student and teacher work (Hartnell-Young and Morriss 1999). The National Board for Professional Teaching Standards (NBPTS) expects teachers seeking certification to submit rigorous portfolios of compelling evidence of meeting standards as part of the certification process (2000 p. 7).

The purpose of the portfolio must be determined before embarking on a portfolio journey. If the stakeholders all know the goal for creating the portfolio before beginning the process, their journey will be successful. Establishing a clear purpose for the portfolio and determining what type of portfolio will best achieve that purpose is the first critical step in the portfolio process.

Examples: Project Academic Purposes

Multiyear Portfolio

(Grades K–2)

1. Recording of student readings from each grade level

2. Two drawings from each grade level, print or digitally scanned

3. Two samples of written work from each grade level (one from the beginning of the year; one from the end of the year)

4. A video clip of one oral presentation from each year.

5. A student-selected "best work" from each year

Integrated Portfolio

Integrates: language arts, social studies, mathematics, science, art

Theme: Criminal Justice

1. Videotape of mock trial of Boo Radley (from *To Kill a Mockingbird*)

2. Analysis of types of capital punishment from a medical perspective

3. Graphs of the number of prisoners on death row in each state, including their race, age, and level of education

4. Journal entry on one day in the life of a death-row prisoner

5. Sketches of scenes from a courtroom or prison

6. Time lines of famous trials in American history

Employment Portfolio

1. Research on three different careers that includes the following:
   - type of training necessary
   - length of training
   - institutions that provide training
   - cost of training
   - anticipated salary

2. Video of a job interview

3. A typed job résumé

4. One collaborative group project

5. List of hobbies, certificates, honors, training, courses, or extracurricular activities

Best Work Portfolio

Subject: American Literature

1. Annotated bibliography of writers associated with the Harlem Renaissance

2. Video clip of debate on which contemporary author deserves the Nobel Prize for Literature

3. A Venn diagram comparing Edgar Allan Poe to Stephen King

4. A critique of Hemingway's novel, *The Sun Also Rises*

5. My Top Ten List of the best American women writers (and a rationale for their ranking)

SkyLight Professional Development

Chapter One

Blackline Masters

Teacher Planner
Portfolio Purpose and Type

Purpose
What are your purposes for using a portfolio?

. . . .

. . . .

. . . .

. . . .

. . . .

Type
What type(s) of portfolio will help fulfill your purpose? Explain why.

. . . .

. . . .

. . . .

. . . .

. . . .

Professional
What would you include in your professional portfolio?

. . . .

. . . .

. . . .

. . . .

. . . .

SkyLight Professional Development • www.skylightedu.com

Standards Portfolio

Select three district or state standards from your curriculum. List three pieces of evidence you could assign students to meet the standards.

Standard:

Evidence:

1. ....

2. ....

3. ....

Standard:

Evidence:

1. ....

2. ....

3. ....

Standard:

Evidence:

1. ....

2. ....

3. ....

Integrated Portfolio

Select a theme (Courage, Rebellion, Space, Environment, the Future, etc.) and brainstorm portfolio entries for each subject area listed in the boxes below.

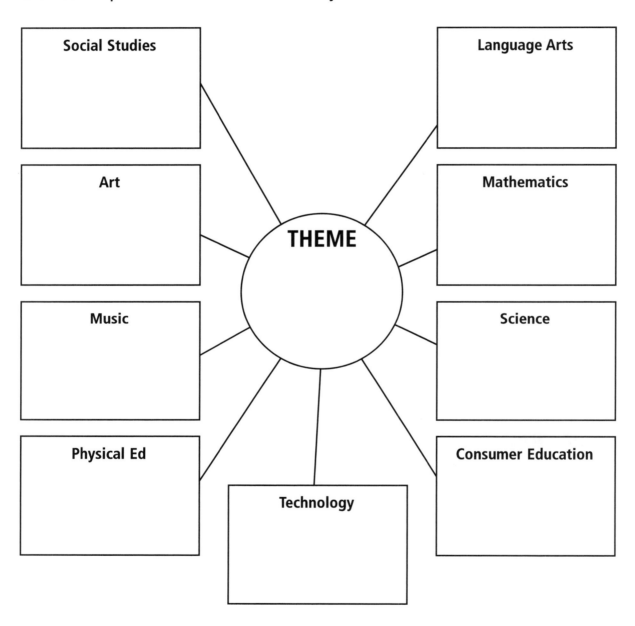

Social Studies

Language Arts

Art

Mathematics

Music

Science

THEME

Physical Ed

Consumer Education

Technology

SkyLight Professional Development • www.skylightedu.com

Multiyear Portfolio

My Portfolio Can Help Me to Tell My Story

Student Name _____ Date _____

1. Label your work according to the grade level.
2. Spread out the work by dates (earliest date to most current date).
3. Select three writing assignments (one from each year).
4. Line them up in order and review them carefully.
5. Answer the following questions about your three samples:
   What major difference do you see?

   _____
   _____

   What surprised you the most?

   _____
   _____

   How have your interests changed?

   _____
   _____

   What skills (handwriting, grammar, spelling, organization, vocabulary, etc.) do you still need to develop more? Why?

   _____
   _____

6. Show your three sample pieces to a peer. Ask for comments about any changes he or she sees.
   Peer Comments: _____

7. Set new goals for yourself.
   Goal One: _____
   Goal Two: _____
   Goal Three: _____

(Adapted from Kate Smith, a teacher at Crow Island School in Winnetka, IL. Used with permission.)

Blackline 1.4

Employment Portfolio

Select items you could include in a portfolio to show to a prospective employer.

Name _____ Date _____

TABLE OF CONTENTS
Academic Skills

1. _____ page _____
2. _____ page _____
3. _____ page _____

Responsibility Skills

4. _____ page _____
5. _____ page _____
6. _____ page _____

Cooperative Skills

7. _____ page _____
8. _____ page _____
9. _____ page _____

SkyLight Professional Development • www.skylightedu.com

Interject Standards and Criteria

Overview

"Standards serve to clarify and raise expectations, and provide a common set of expectations" (Kendall and Marzano 1997, p. 5). Standards provide guidelines to help teachers focus on clear outcomes for all students to achieve. Many districts and states developed content and performance standards for student learning that define what students should know and be able to do as a result of their schooling. Standards serve as road maps to help educators focus on the critical areas students need to master in order to move to the next level of learning.

Foriska (1998) talks about the "unevenness" or gap in talents, skills, knowledge, and experience students bring with them to the inclusive classroom. He states that "although some students come with this gap in their abilities, schools have traditionally been organized to provide education in a 'random' manner that can further add to the unevenness of student development" (p. 5). By the same token, students who master skills quickly endure repetitive lessons while other students struggle with acquiring the skills. Teachers have the challenge to differentiate the instruction to meet the needs of a diverse student population. Students who score low on standardized tests become frustrated, embarrassed, and oftentimes disruptive whereas students who master the standards quickly become bored or disengaged by the monotonous repetition and drilling of skills they already know.

Introduction

In addition to being challenged by the wide variety of student ability, teachers are overwhelmed by the expanding curriculum. They are confused about what to teach in depth and what to cover quickly. The standards help teachers focus on the key skills and concepts students need to know to build the foundation of learning as well as to prepare them for standardized tests. Figure 2.1 list ways standards benefit students, educators, and parents if they serve as guideposts for learning opportunities, not mandated prescriptions for "one size fits all" learning.

Digital Connection

The digital portfolio provides an impressive means of presenting both visual and audio products from student engagement in learning processes that incorporate multiple intelligences. These products are stored as files on zip disks or CDs or as Web pages on school Web sites.

Standards as Guideposts

Standards can benefit students by helping educators to:

S ynthesize educational goals

T arget student achievement

A lign curriculum systemically

N otify the public of results

D etermine criteria for quality work

A nalyze data

R efocus instructional methodology

D edicate resources to professional development

S erve the needs of a diverse population

Figure 2.1   From *How to Assess Authentic Learning,* 3rd edition, p. 16, by K. Burke. © 1999 by SkyLight Training and Publishing Inc. Used with permission.

Standards also help educators agree upon common vocabulary and goals that transcend textbooks and curriculum guides. Regardless of where students live, what resources are available, or which teacher they have, students and parents know the knowledge, skills, and processes delineated by content area experts around the country are important for each student at each grade level to master for success. The universality of most standards cuts across geographical locations.

Educators in each subject area work to achieve consensus, in most cases, on the essential learnings students must know and be able to apply. Even though standards typically reinforce the best practices of effective teaching, the process of implementing and addressing standards varies. Carr and Harris (2001) state that "some standards are being taught but not assessed, assessed but not taught, or inconsistently taught and assessed within or across grade levels" (p. 5). Some states and districts provide teachers with the standards, examples of work that demonstrate the students have met the standards, and indicators or benchmarks that should be included if the work meets or exceeds standards. Often, however, teachers generate their own assignments and assessments to meet the standards. Therefore, even though the standards themselves are similar from district to district and from state to state, their implementation and assessment varies. Figure 2.2 demonstrates how standards for various disciplines can be taught and assessed. (A blackline master for standards and assessment planning is provided at the end of this chapter, Blackline 2.1).

Standards-Based Portfolio System

Teachers who require students to save copies of their work have accomplished the first step in the portfolio process. But merely collecting assignments is not much different from having students keep a notebook or a folder of their work. The work is included—but how does anyone know if the work shows improvement, demonstrates quality, or meets or exceeds the standards? For a standards portfolio to be meaningful, a checklist or a rubric should accompany the student's work to indicate whether or not the student meets the

> Standards help educators agree upon a common vocabulary and common goals that transcend textbooks and curriculum guides.

Sample Standards and Assessments

Language Arts
The student produces a narrative account.

Assessments
1. A news account of an event in history
2. A biographical account of a famous American
3. A travel diary of a trip

Mathematics
The student demonstrates and applies geometric concepts involving points, lines, planes, and space.

Assessments
1. Drawings of two-dimensional shapes
2. Drawings of circle and sphere, square and cube, triangle and pyramid
3. Pictures of art, advertising, construction that show geometric figures

Health
The student can explain the basic principles of health promotion, illness prevention, and safety.

Assessments
1. Pamphlet related to a specific disease (symptoms, preventions, treatments)
2. Report on safety methods that reduce risks (wearing seat belts, wearing helmets, using sunscreen)

Science
The student knows and applies the concepts, principles, and processes of scientific inquiry.

Assessments
1. Formulate questions on a science topic and select five steps to answer questions.
2. Collect data and construct a chart to display data.
3. Give an oral report on reasonable explanations.

Figure 2.2

standard. If the student does not meet the standard, the teacher must also mark specific indicators describing what the student needs to do in order to improve.

The best works portfolio allows students to select their very best work, which helps students to improve their self-esteem and impress their parents at back-to-school night. The standards portfolio, on the other hand, demands more rigor. The steps educators take to achieve this rigor appear below.

STEPS FOR A STANDARDS-BASED PORTFOLIO ENTRY

1. Select the learning standard.
2. Determine the assignment, project, or performance by which students will demonstrate their ability to meet the standard.
3. Create a criteria or descriptor checklist to guide students in the process.
4. Develop a rubric or score sheet to describe the levels students need to achieve to meet or exceed the standard.

Organizing Portfolio Entries

Teachers need a plan to help students organize their work into a standards portfolio. Students can organize the loose assignments more efficiently if they are each given a hanging folder. Students write their names on the outside of the hanging folder and insert separate folders, each a different color and already labeled with each

standard. These folders are labeled so that students and teachers can file each assignment according to the standard it addresses. Teachers can use file cabinets or milk crates for storing the hanging folders.

When items are sent home for parent review, students are instructed to bring them back to include in their folders. Rough drafts along with final copies, graded papers, rewrites, and pictures of projects and performances are among the items included in the portfolio. The portfolio offers concrete evidence to show the standard was addressed; the student-produced document proves he completed the assignment and the checklist or rubric demonstrates to what degree he met the standard.

One method to document students' meeting each standard is to write the specific standard at the top of each entry.

E2c. The student produces a narrative account.

```
Mary Ortiz
9/5/01


My First Snowball Fight
I was five years old when my parents moved
to New York from Florida, and I first saw
snow! I was asleep in the backseat . . .
```

Middle school language arts teachers—responsible for helping students meet five standards related to reading, writing, speaking, listening, and viewing—can require students to list the appropriate standard at the top of each piece of work and file them in separate folders. This type of accountability system helps teachers, parents, and students monitor progress to make sure all of the standards are taught and assessed.

Standards and Criteria Checklists

Some state standards provide educators with specific descriptors, indicators, or criteria that demonstrate what needs to be included in a work sample. Other districts and states provide only the standard, which is sometimes very broad and generic. In this case, teachers must generate their own criteria to help students complete the assignment.

Specific Standards

When districts or states provide specific standards, teachers need to create their own descriptor checklists to guide students to meet the standard. Using the specifics from the standards, teachers can generate their own criteria to guide their teaching. One of the specific writing skills under New York City Standard E-2 Writing involves writing a narrative account. The standard states that the student produces a narrative account (fictional or autobiographical) that

- engages the reader by establishing a context, creating a point of view, and otherwise developing reader interest;
- establishes a situation, plot, point of view, setting, and conflict (and for autobiography, the significance of events and of conclusions that can be drawn from those events);
- creates an organizing structure;
- includes sensory details and concrete language to develop plot and character;
- excludes extraneous details and inconsistencies;
- uses a range of appropriate strategies such as dialogue, tension or suspense, naming, and specific narrative action (e.g., movement, gestures, expressions); and
- provides a sense of closure to the writing.
  (Board of Education of the City of New York 1997)

The performance descriptors provide the criteria teachers should use to help students produce the narrative account. Since the descriptors might be overwhelming, teachers cluster or chunk the criteria into sequential order so students progress in a logical order and complete one step at a time (see Figure 2.3).

Digital Connection

As students learn about state standards and become skillful in applying their own benchmarks of learning to these standards, the digital portfolio enables them to link their artifacts to the standards posted on state Web sites.

Clustered Checklist for Narrative Account

Performance Descriptors	Not Yet 0	Some Evidence 1
Engages Reader		
Context of story		
Reader interest		
Establishes a Situation		
Plot		
Point of view		
Setting		
Conflict		
Creates an Organizing Structure		
Topic sentence		
Support sentence		
Transitions		
Motif/theme		
Symbolism		
Develops Complex Characters		
Protagonist		
Antagonist		
Dialogue		
Creates Sensory Details		
Descriptive language		
Figurative language		

Figure 2.3

Checklists as Guideposts

Standards that include specific indicators and criteria facilitate the creation of checklists because they provide teachers with key words or concepts to include in the checklists. Teachers can also create user-friendly checklists that guide students in the completion of a task. For example, teachers in Community School District 4 in New York developed a checklist to help their fourth grade students produce a report on Native American Indians of New York state (Figure 2.4). This checklist demonstrates how teachers can guide students through each step in the process to write a research report.

Since writing a report requires research, the students first have to check off and sometimes write in the information they have gathered. If students complete the entire checklist, they will do a better job on their written report. Often, teachers staple the checklist to the student's work before placing it in the portfolio. The checklist provides a way to monitor progress toward completing the final task.

Rubrics

The major weakness of attaching only a checklist to the portfolio entry is that it may not indicate the quality of the work. Students may include an item on the checklist, but the item may not exhibit quality. A student may include a topic sentence, but what if it is poorly written and has no relationship to the paragraph? A rubric takes the checklist to a higher level. A rubric is a scoring guide that spells out what makes an effective topic sentence and, most importantly, whether or not that topic sentence meets or exceeds the standards. On a rubric, the student can see exactly what he or she has to do to move forward on the continuum toward quality work. The narrative writing rubric (Figure 2.5) utilizes the clustered checklist in Figure 2.3 to determine criteria, but expands the criteria by generating descriptors and ratings for each criteria so students know how they rate and what they need to do to improve their narrative piece.

Research Report Checklist
(GRADE 4)

New York City Language Arts Standard
Produce a report of information.

New York State Social Studies Standard
Native American Indians of New York State

Assignment   Complete a research report on New York State Native Americans—Algonquin or Iroquois

Research

Gather information from three different sources.

___Internet   ___Historical fiction
___Social studies text   ___Maps/charts/time lines
___Resource books   ___Other:_____

Identify important ideas and cultural information.

___Language   ___Dress
___Food   ___Tradition
___Education   ___Religion
___Population   ___Activities

Understand facts about geographic location.

___Where did they live? _____
___What kinds of homes did they have? _____
___When did their culture flourish? _____

Organize information.

___Notes   ___Graphic organizer
___Outline   ___Charts

Present Information in Written Form

___Title page with artwork/graphics
___Outline
___Five Paragraphs

(continued on next page)

Figure 2.4

Paragraph Organization

PARAGRAPH 1 Who?_____

Main idea_____

Three supporting details _____

_____

_____

PARAGRAPH 2 When did their culture flourish? _____

Main idea_____

Supporting details _____

_____

PARAGRAPH 3 Where?_____

– Location on New York State map _____

– Effect of location on lives _____

Supporting details _____

_____

PARAGRAPH 4 Culture—Main idea _____

– Three important ideas _____

– Supporting details for each idea _____

_____

_____

PARAGRAPH 5 Conclusion

– Summary of main ideas _____

– Influence on our culture _____

– What did you learn? _____

_____

Bibliography

– Number of sources

– Types of sources

Contributed by Phyllis Dichek, Brunilda Caceres, and Sandra Rinaldo, PS146, Community School District 4, New York. Used with permission.

Figure 2.4 (continued)

Rubric for Narrative Writing

Criteria	Below Standards 1	Almost Meets Standards 2	Meets Standards 3	Exceeds Standards 4
Engages Reader				
• Context	No context	Context is confusing	Context sets the scene for the story	Context develops a framework for the story
• Reader Interest	Does not engage reader	Attempts to engage reader	Captures the reader's attention	Grips the reader throughout narrative
Establishes a Situation				
• Plot	No evidence of plot	Plot is confusing and/or doesn't make sense	Plot is developed coherently	Plot provides surprising twists
• Point of View	Vague point of view	Varies from 1st, 2nd, to 3rd person	Shifts from 1st person to 3rd person on occasion	Uses appropriate point of view consistently and effectively
• Setting	Not provided	Provides place or time	Provides place and time	Vividly describes both place and time
• Conflict	No conflict	Rising action	• Rising action • Climax	• Rising action • Climax • Denouement
Creates an Organizing Structure				
• Topic Sentence	None	Wrong main idea	Correct and controlling main idea	Clear and powerful main idea
• Support Sentence	Sentences do not relate to topic sentence	1 supporting sentence related to topic	2 supporting sentences related to topic	3 or more well-written supporting sentences
• Transitions	No transitions	Basic transitions (and, but. . .) used appropriately	Varied transitions (however, moreover, therefore. . .) used	Skillful use of transitional words and phrases to connect ideas
• Motif/Theme	No evidence	Vague theme—not fully developed	Theme woven throughout	Theme appropriately conveys author's message
• Symbolism	No symbols	Vague use of one symbol—not fully developed	1 to 2 appropriate symbols woven throughout	1 to 2 effective symbols that contribute significantly to the meaning of the story

Figure 2.5 (continued on next page)

Rubric for Narrative Writing

Criteria	Below Standards 1	Almost Meets Standards 2	Meets Standards 3	Exceeds Standards 4
Develops Complex Characters				
• Protagonist	Not fully developed	Stereotypical "good guy" (no surprises)	Fully developed main character	Complex and empathetic main character
• Antagonist	Not fully developed	Stereotypical "bad guy" (no surprises)	Fully developed foil to main character	Complex foil to main character
• Dialogue	Little or not dialogue among characters	Stilted dialogue that does not fully develop characters	Realistic dialogue appropriate to characters—advances plot line	Colorful dialogue with use of appropriate dialect, idioms, slang
Creates Sensory Details				
• Descriptive Language	Lacks specific descriptions	Word choice is bland and nondescript	Use of descriptive adjectives	Vivid use of descriptive words that "paint a picture" in the mind
• Figurative Language	No figurative language	Use of simile or metaphor	Use of simile and metaphor	Creative use of similes and metaphors
• Concrete Language	Nondescript language	Use of appropriate vocabulary	Action verbs and colorful adjectives	Vivid word usage enhances narrative
Closure				
• Foreshadowing	No evidence	1 obvious hint	2 hints	3 or more subtle hints
• Story Ending	No ending/or inappropriate ending—no foreshadowing	Unsatisfying ending—loose ends (weak foreshadowing)	Ending provides closure to story—evidence of foreshadowing	Cleverly foreshadowed surprise ending

Points	Scale
19–25	Below Standards
26–45	Almost Meets Standards
46–65	Meets Standards
66–76	Exceeds Standards

Comments: _____

Signed: _____   Date: _____

Figure 2.5 (continued)

Portfolio vs. Collection of "Stuff"

In today's age of accountability, collecting student work, placing it in a folder, and showing it to administrators and parents is not sufficient proof that the teacher has covered the curriculum and the student has mastered the standards. A standards portfolio contains student work correlated to curriculum goals, aligned to standards, and assessed with checklists and rubrics. It provides concrete evidence of the students' progress toward meeting or exceeding goals. The standards-based portfolio, therefore, ensures a more systematic and structured approach to assessment and provides a rich opportunity for monitoring student learning.

As Popham (1999) states, "Ideally, teachers who adapt portfolios in their classrooms will make the ongoing collection and appraisal of students' work a central focus of the instructional program rather than a peripheral activity whereby students occasionally gather up their work to convince a teacher's supervisor or students' parents that good things have been going on in class" (p. 182). Portfolios—especially standards-based portfolios—provide more than a scrapbook to share on back-to-school night. They document students' learning and support the grading system that evaluates student's progress or lack of progress in achieving academic goals. Portfolios also help teachers monitor their own effectiveness in teaching skills necessary for students to achieve deep understanding of essential learnings.

Examples: Interject Standards and Criteria

Standards and Assessments

SOCIAL SCIENCE
Standard: Understand the development of significant political events.
Assessments:
1. Create a cause and effect graphic organizer for the American Revolution.
2. Compare and contrast the facts of an historical event and a fictional story about the event.

FINE ARTS—DANCE
Standard: Apply skills and knowledge necessary to create and perform in the arts.
Assessments:
1. Create a dance that demonstrates coordination, balance, and rhythmic response.
2. Demonstrate step patterns from different dance styles and forms.

FOREIGN LANGUAGE
Standard: Understand oral communication in the target language.
Assessments:
1. Rewrite a Spanish folktale in English.
2. Write and illustrate a recipe in the target language.

TECHNOLOGY
Standard: Use technology to locate, select, and manage information.
Assessments:
1. Create a reference list of Internet sources on an assigned topic.
2. Research a topic using three types of media.

Persuasive Speech Checklist

STANDARD *Students will deliver a persuasive speech*

Criteria Performance Indicators	Not Yet 0	Some Evidence 1
Organization		
• Hook to grab attention		
• Smooth transitions		
• Effective closing		
Content		
• Accurate facts		
• Appropriate quotations		
• Credible sources		
Delivery		
• Voice projection		
• Eye contact with audience		
• Appropriate gestures		
Persuasiveness		
• Logical arguments		
• Convincing case		
• Empassioned appeal		

Mathematics Graph Checklist

STANDARD *Students should select, create, and use appropriate graphical representatives of data.*

Criteria Performance Indicators	Not Yet 0	Sometimes 1	Frequently 2
Titles and Neatness			
• Axes and main title labeled			
• Accurate points on line graph			
• Axes numbers correct			
• Neatly used ruler and color pencils			
• Includes a key			
Equations			
• Break-even correct with work			
• Profit correct with work shown			
• No grammar or spelling errors			
Working Together			
• Worked well with partners			

Adapted from Jean Tucknott, Eisenhower Jr. High, Schaumburg District #54, Illinois. Used with permission.

Autobiographical Checklist

STANDARD *The student produces an autobiographical account*

Criteria Performance Indicators	Not Yet 0	Some Evidence 1
Structure/Organization		
• Does your story have a begining that hooks the reader?		
• Does your story have three paragraphs in the body?		
Content		
• Does your story have a plot? (5 Ws)		
• Does your story have logical sequence?		
• Does your story have dialogue?		
• Does your story have an ending?		
Mechanics		
• Are all your sentences complete?		
• Did you capitalize words correctly?		
• Did you check your punctuation?		
• Did you have current subject/verb agreement?		

SkyLight Professional Development

Chapter Two

Blackline Masters

Teacher Planner
Standards and Assessments

Teacher:_____ Subject/Levels:_____ Date:_____

Directions: Select a content lesson and list the curriculum objectives and standards the lesson will address. Brainstorm three methods of assessment to evaluate student performance.

Content Lesson:_____

Curriculum Objectives:

_____

_____

_____

Standards:

_____

_____

_____

Assessments:

1. _____

2. _____

3. _____

Research Report Checklist

Name:_____   Date:_____

Criteria	No Evidence 0	Evidence 1
Research		
• 3 Types of Sources		
• 10 Notecards		
• 5 Bibliography Cards		
Organization		
• Outline (3 Roman Numerals)		
• Introduction (1 Paragraph)		
• Body (3+ Paragraphs)		
• Conclusion (1 Paragraph)		
• Bibliography (5 Sources)		
Content		
• Thesis Statement (take a stand)		
• 4–5 Pro Arguments (support stand)		
• 2–3 Con Arguments (give opposition)		
• 5 Quotes from Experts (APA form)		

Comments: _____

_____

_____

_____

_____

_____

Scale:
10–12 points = A
8–9 points   = B
5–7 points   = C
below 7   = Not Yet

Grade: _____

Blackline 2.2

Clustered Checklist—Standard

Name:_____ Date:_____

Standard:_____

Performance Indicators:_____

Cluster the indicators into five areas.

Criteria/Performance Indicators	Not Yet 0	Some Evidence 1
•		
•		
•		
•		
•		
•		
•		
•		
•		
•		
•		
•		
•		
•		
•		

Comments:

Blackline 2.3

SkyLight Professional Development • www.skylightedu.com

Clustered Checklist For Task

Name:_____ Date:_____

Task:_____

Standard: _____

Cluster the indicators into five areas.

Criteria/Performance Indicators	Not Yet 0	Some Evidence 1
_____		
•		
•		
•		
_____		
•		
•		
•		
_____		
•		
•		
•		
_____		
•		
•		
•		
_____		
•		
•		
•		

Comments:

Blackline 2.4

Connect to Curriculum Goals

Overview

Even though the modern standards movement in education began around 1995 with Diane Ravitch's publication of *National Standards in American Education: A Citizen's Guide,* educators have addressed curriculum goals and objectives for many years. One of the major goals of states and school systems is to align the high-stakes standardized tests to the standards, the curriculum, and the assessments. These elements must be correlated in order for the data collected from standardized tests to be valid. Before the standards movement, teachers relied on their curriculum guides to help them determine what and sometimes when to teach objectives. The scope and sequence of the guides provided a road map for teachers and helped them determine what students needed to know at each grade level. Unfortunately, sometimes the objectives numbered in the hundreds and teachers spent too much time engaged in management by objectives rather than actual teaching. The curriculum guides, however, are important components because they often supply the specific content that is the core of the standards.

Introduction

There are some educators who fear that standards and behavioral objectives are too numerous and narrow and, therefore, reduce teaching to an accounting nightmare. State documents outline hundreds of bits of information that create expectations for content coverage at the expense of in-depth learning. Linda Darling-Hammond (1997) warns that "covering" the content makes it impossible for students to acquire the understanding they need to apply ideas. They cover so many facts so quickly that they have no time to create the meaningful projects and performances that demonstrate their understanding.

Many states have created curriculum frameworks to embody new content and performance standards to provide directions for schools to meet the needs of their students. The curriculum could be the "bridge between standards at one end and what happens in the classroom at the other" (Darling-Hammond 1997, p. 230).

Digital Connection

The digital portfolio provides an effective means for students to demonstrate their recognition of connections between topics and ideas. The ease of linking electronic entries within the digital portfolio promotes students' understanding of the natural integration between subjects.

Not all students fit into the scope and the sequence presented in curriculum guides. Teachers need to meet students where they are and move them forward. Performance tasks allow teachers to create learning experiences that cluster standards and objectives, engage the students, allow for individual differences, and provide student work that meets both standards and curriculum goals. Thoughtful teachers use the curriculum not as an end in itself, but as a means to achieve the lifelong goals of communication, problem solving, decision making, accessing information, and socialization skills.

Performance Tasks

Performance tasks relate knowledge to real-life applications. These umbrella problem scenarios require students to engage in a variety of integrated activities in order to achieve an end product. The task addresses multiple standards and curricular goals and involves whole-class work, small-group work, and individual work. Lewin and Shoemaker (1998) state that a task can be completed in one class period, two to three class periods, or a week or more. In their definition, a performance task has the following key characteristics:

- Students have some choice in selecting or shaping the task.
- The task requires both the elaboration of core knowledge content and the use of key processes.
- The task has an explicit scoring system.
- The task is designed for an audience larger than the teacher; that is, others outside the classroom would find value in the work.
- The task is carefully crafted to measure what it purports to measure.

> From *Great Performances: Creating Classroom-Based Assessment Tasks* by Larry Lewin and Betty Jean Shoemaker. Alexandria, VA: Association for Supervision and Curriculum Development. © 1998 ASCD. Reprinted with permission. All rights reserved.

PERFORMANCE TASK:
An assessment with a stated scoring system that addresses multiple standards and goals.

Figure 3.1 is an example of a Language Arts Performance Task; Figure 3.2 is an example of a Mathematics Performance Task; and Figure 3.3 shows a checklist for the individual assignments.

Performance Task Plan

Subject: <u>Writing—Persuasive</u>   Grade: <u>4</u>
Curriculum: State History

Standards:
1. Compose well-organized and coherent writing for specific purposes and audiences
2. Speak effectively using appropriate language
3. Use correct grammar, spelling, punctuation, capitalization, and sentence structure.

Performance Task
Your class has been selected by our Governor to prepare an advertising campaign to attract visitors to our state. Your marketing campaign should include a poster, brochure, Web page, radio commercial, and television commercial. Be prepared to present your campaign strategies to the Governor on_____.

Group Work

One	Two	Three	Four	Five
Create a poster advertising our state	Create a brochure for tourists	Design a Web page about our state	Create a one-minute radio commercial	Create a one-minute television commercial

Individual Work Correlated to Standards
1. Each student will write a persuasive letter essay convincing a friend in another state to visit our state this summer.
2. Each student will deliver a 5-minute persuasive speech to the Governor explaining why people should vacation in our state.

Methods of Assessment
1. Criteria Checklists for five group projects
2. Rubric developed by students to assess persuasive letter
3. Rubric developed by teacher to assess oral presentation

Figure 3.1

Performance Task Plan

Subject: Mathematics/Lang. Arts   Grade: 6
Curriculum: Making predictions from data

Standards:

1. Organize and display data using charts, circle graphs, bar graphs, and double-line graphs.
2. Make predictions and decisions based on data.
3. Write a persuasive letter.

Performance Task

You have been asked by the new owner of Acme Music Store to conduct a survey of 150 people of different age groups in our community to determine what type of music they would buy. Be prepared to present a circle graph representing percentages for responses, a bar graph depicting the relationship between age groups, a double-line graph showing the relationship between gender and musical preference, and a prediction from your graphs about what inventory to stock.

Group Work

One	Two	Three	Four
Write the survey using categories such as classical, rock, etc.	Construct a bar graph depicting the relationship between age groups and musical preference.	Construct a double-line graph showing the relationship between males and females and musical preference.	Make a prediction from your graphs about what inventory to stock.

Individual Work Correlated to Standards

1. Write a persuasive letter to the new owner of Acme Music convincing him to stock music that the community would be willing to buy.
2. Using six categories (hip hop, country, classical, rock, blues, spiritual), design a circle graph poster representing responses from the people interviewed.

Methods of Assessment

1. Checklist to assess each group's work
2. Rubric to assess the persuasive letter
3. Checklist to assess individual circle graphs

Figure 3.3   Adapted from teachers in Warren County High School in Tennessee. Used with permission.

Checklist for Circle Graph

Design a circle graph poster representing the percentages for all responses from survey.

Indicators for Circle Graph	No (0)	Yes (1)
Surveyed 50 people from all three age groups 12–16 17–21 over 21		
Calculated percentages correctly		
Used no more than 6 categories of music		
Completed circle graph (labeled, divided correctly, etc.)		
Included title of circle graph		
Used different colors for each category		
Neat appearance		
Accurate information		
Paragraph description incuded		
Handed in on due date		

Comments:

Figure 3.3

Adapted from teachers in Warren County High School in Tennessee. Used with permission.

SkyLight Professional Development

Unit Plans—Multiple Intelligences Portfolio

Performance tasks cluster the standards into meaningful experiences that students understand because of their correlation to real-life experiences. Authentic tasks also motivate students and provide a realistic context for learning. In addition to performance tasks, educators design integrated units that cluster groups of curriculum objectives and standards and include a variety of assignments and assessments that meet students' diverse learning styles. One method of creating a unit portfolio involves using Howard Gardner's (1983, 1993) theory of multiple intelligences. (See Figure 3.4 for concepts and words associated with each intelligence.) Students have a choice in selecting some assignments, but they are required to show they have met the standards and curriculum goals.

UNIT PLANS:
A cluster of curriculum objectives and standards into a variety of assignments with diverse assessments

A multiple intelligences portfolio includes entries that represent the eight intelligences. Students collect:

- logs, journals, and reflections to depict verbal/linguistic and intrapersonal intelligences;
- a Venn diagram to depict visual/spatial intelligence;
- a computer program to depict logical/mathematical intelligence;
- a video of a group performance to depict bodily/kinesthetic and interpersonal intelligences;
- a rap song to represent musical/rhythmic intelligence; and
- a classification chart of leaves to represent naturalist intelligence.

Students select items that showcase their talents and teachers select items that address curriculum goals. This type of portfolio contains multiple entries that demands students to stretch their talents and expand their repertoire of products and processes. Requiring students to expand their intelligences enhances their creativity and helps teachers meet students' diverse learning styles. Figure 3.5 classifies the various learning experiences and assessments by intelligences, Figure 3.6 is a sample unit portfolio on space, and Figure 3.7 is a sample unit portfolio for Greek mythology (also see the Appendix for a completed portfolio on Greek mythology). You may use Blackline 3.4 (at the end of this chapter) to create a plan for your own multiple intelligences portfolio.

Gardner's Multiple Intelligences

Visual/Spatial
images, graphics, drawings, sketches, maps, charts, doodles, pictures, spatial orientation, puzzles, designs, looks, appeal, mind's eye, imagination, visualization, dreams, nightmares, films, and videos

Logical/Mathematical
reasoning, deductive and inductive logic, facts, data, information, spreadsheets, databases, sequencing, ranking, organizing, analyzing, proofs, conclusions, judging, evaluations, and assessments

Verbal/Linguistic
words, wordsmiths, speaking, writing, listening, reading, papers, essays, poems, plays, narratives, lyrics, spelling, grammar, foreign languages, memos, bulletins, newsletters, newspapers, e-mail, faxes, speeches, talks, dialogues, and debates

Musical/Rhythmic
music, rhythm, beat, melody, tunes, allegro, pacing, timbre, tenor, soprano, opera, baritone, symphony, choir, chorus, madrigals, rap, rock, rhythm, blues, jazz, classical, folk, ads, and jingles

Bodily/Kinesthetic
activity, action, experiential, hands-on, experiments, try, do, perform, play, drama, sports, throw, toss, catch, jump, twist, twirl, assemble, disassemble, form, re-form, manipulate, touch, feel, immerse, and participate

Interpersonal
interact, communicate, converse, share, understand, empathize, sympathize, reach out, care, talk, whisper, laugh, cry, shudder, socialize, meet, greet, lead, follow, gangs, clubs, charisma, crowds, gatherings, and twosomes

Intrapersonal
self, solitude, meditate, think, create, brood, reflect, envision, journal, self-assess, set goals, plot, plan, dream, write, fiction, nonfiction, poetry, affirmations, lyrics, songs, screenplays, commentaries, introspection, and inspection

Naturalist
nature, natural, environment, listen, watch, observe, classify, categorize, discern patterns, appreciate, hike, climb, fish, hunt, dive, photograph, trees, leaves, animals, living things, flora, fauna, ecosystem, sky, grass, mountains, lakes, and rivers

Figure 3.4   Adapted from *Integrating Curricula with Multiple Intelligences: Teams, Themes, & Threads,* p. 8, by R. Fogarty and J. Stoehr. ©1995 by IRI/SkyLight Training and Publishing, Inc. Used with permission.

SkyLight Professional Development

Learning, Experiences, and Assessments Classified by Multiple Intelligences*

Verbal/ Linguistic	Logical/ Mathematical	Visual/ Spatial	Bodily/ Kinesthetic
• tape recordings of readings • reactions to guest speakers • autobiographies • reactions to films or videos • scripts for radio shows • lists of books read • annotated bibliographies	• puzzles • patterns and their relationships • mathematical operations • formulas/abstract symbols • analogies • time lines • Venn diagrams • original word problems	• artwork • photographs • math manipulatives • graphic organizers • posters, charts, graphics, pictures • illustrations • sketches • props for plays • storyboards	• field trips • role playing • learning centers • labs • sports/games • simulations • presentations • dances

Musical/Rhythmic	Interpersonal	Intrapersonal	Naturalist
• background music in class • songs for books, countries, people • raps, jingles, cheers, poems • musical mnemonics • choral readings • tone patterns • music and dance of different cultures • musical symbols	• group videos, films, filmstrips • team computer programs • cooperative task trios • round robins • jigsaws • wraparounds • e-mail • class and group discussions • group projects • group presentations	• problem-solving strategies • goal setting • reflective logs • divided journals • metacognitive reflections • independent reading • silent reflection time • self-evaluations	• outdoor education • environmental studies • field trips • nature photographs • research on ecosystems • debates on environmental issues • poems about nature

* Many activities and assessments overlap into several intelligences.

Figure 3.5

Adapted from *How to Assess Authentic Learning*, 3rd Edition, p. 47, by K. Burke.
© 1999 SkyLight Training and Publishing Inc. Used with permission.

Unit Portfolio: Space

Standards: 1. Use reading, writing, listening, and speaking skills to research and apply information for specific purposes.
2. Understand the facts and unifying concepts of earth/space sciences.
3. Identify and explain ways that science and technology influence the direction of people's lives.

Verbal/ Linguistic	Logical/ Mathematical	Visual/ Spatial	Bodily/ Kinesthetic
• Develop a list of vocabulary words for space. • Write a joke book for space creatures. • Write a short story set on a planet. • Keep a diary about a trip you took in space. • Research a planet.	• Graph the distances of planets from the sun or other planets. • Calculate the length of a trip to the moon traveling at 100 miles per hour. • Classify planets by temperature and size. • Calculate the cost of fuel needed to reach the moon.	• Draw a picture of what you think a Martian looks like. • Make a model of the solar system. • Make a clay sculpture of a planet. • Create a Venn diagram comparing Earth and Mars.	• Act out the astronauts' first steps on the moon. • Simulate the sun or the orbits of all the planets. • Create a sport that would be popular in space (with no gravity). • Demonstrate gravity in an experiment.

Musical/Rhythmic	Interpersonal	Intrapersonal	Naturalist
• Write a planetary anthem for one of the planets. • Write a rap song for one of the planets. • Create a new dance named *Space Walk*. • Write poetry to the music from *2001, A Space Odyssey*.	• Interview E.T. about his trip to Earth. • Role play the parts of each member of a space crew. • Plan a joint space expedition with another country. • Practice peer mediation with an alien. • Give a speech persuading others to explore space.	• Meditate on being the first person to walk on the moon. • Describe how it would feel to be the first student in space. • Tell how you would feel if you did not see sunlight for a long time. • Write a letter to an astronaut.	• Classify plants found in space. • Identify rock samples found on planets. • Forecast the weather for a planet. • Plan a nature week on a planet. • Create a survival guide for life on Mars.

Standards Pieces	Item 1	Item 2	Item 3	Item 4
	Research report on planet	*Speech on space exploration*	*Survival guide*	*Gravity experiment*

Student Choice	Item 5	Item 6	Item 7	Item 8

Figure 3.6

Adapted from teachers, Cobb County, Georgia. Used with permission

SkyLight Professional Development

Unit Portfolio: Greek Mythology

Standards:
1. Communicate in writing to describe, inform, persuade, and entertain.
2. Demonstrate comprehension of a broad range of reading materials.
3. Use reading, writing, listening, and speaking skills to research and apply information for specific purposes.

Verbal/ Linguistic	Logical/ Mathematical	Visual/ Spatial	Bodily/ Kinesthetic
• Read *The Iliad.* • Read *The Odyssey.* • Read Edith Hamilton's *Mythology.* • Write an original myth to explain a scientific mystery. • Write poems about mythology. • Write a eulogy for a fallen Greek or Trojan warrior.	• Use a Venn diagram to compare the Greeks and the Trojans. • Create original story problems that can incorporate Pythagorean theorem. • Draw a family tree of the twelve Olympians. • Complete a timeline of Odysseus' trip home from Troy.	• Draw the battle plan for the Greeks' attack on Troy. • Draw Mt. Olympus. • Sketch the Greek gods and goddesses. • Create a video of the Olympic games. • Draw items that relate to mythology.	• Act out a Greek trajedy. • Recreate some of the Olympic events. • Act out a myth. • Create a dance for the forest nymphs. • Reenact the battle scene between Hector and Achilles.

Musical/Rhythmic	Interpersonal	Intrapersonal	Naturalist
• Write a song for a lyre. • Pretend you are Apollo, God of Music, and CEO of Motown. • Select music that correlates to each god or goddess.	• Interview Helena about her role in the Trojan War. • Work in a group to create a digital crossword puzzle about mythology.	• Pretend you are a Greek soldier away from home for ten years. Keep a diary of your thoughts. • Write a journal about how you would feel if you were Prometheus chained to a rock.	• Using scientific data predict how long it will take before anything grows after the Greeks destroy Troy and sow the fields with salt. • Describe the animals and plants on Mt. Olympus.

	Item 1	Item 2	Item 3	Item 4
Standards Pieces	Research report on Trojan War	Persuasive essay supporting Greeks' strategies	Book report on *The Odyssey*	Original poem on mythology
	Item 5	**Item 6**	**Item 7**	**Item 8**
Student Choice				

Figure 3.7

Adapted from *How to Assess Authentic Learning*, 3rd Edition, p. 49, by K. Burke.
©1999 by SkyLight Training and Publishing Inc. Used with permission.

Both performance tasks and multiple intelligences units lend themselves to using portfolios because portfolios capture more than grades on a test. These curriculum units are designed to "engage students in exploring and deepening their understanding of important ideas" (Wiggins and McTighe 1998, p. 3). The units themselves deepen the students' understanding of key concepts, but the design of the assessments reveal the extent of their understanding and their ability to meet the standards. By using checklists, rubrics, and unit portfolios to assess their knowledge, skills, and understanding, teachers showcase the results. Portfolios provide the framework for showcasing the multiple talents, skills, and interests of the students and add a multi-dimensional depth to the evaluation process.

Examples: Connect to Curriculum Goals

Language Arts

Standard: Students will listen, speak, read, and write for information, understanding, and social interaction.

Performance Task:

The principal has selected your class to create an orientation program for all students new to our school. The program should include a welcome letter, a tour of the school, an information booklet, a skit, and a picture book of the school's history. Be prepared to present your entire program to the administration on _September 28_.

Biology

Standard: Students will investigate the diversity of organisms by exploring diverse environments.

Performance Task:

Your team will be sent on a survival training mission to a remote biome. You need to research your biome and prepare your team to survive for six weeks. Prepare a map of the area, graphs of rainfalls and temperatures, an analysis of food available, and a chart of plants and animals indigenous to the area. You will present your data to the new recruits on _October 8_

Mathematics

Standards: Operatives and procedures, measurement, statistics and probability

Objective: Geometry operations

The city council has selected our class to bid on the landscaping design of a new garden for the town square. The project will include a scale drawing of the design, a cost estimation, a time line, a presentation to the city council, and an official proposal and contract. Be prepared to present your proposal at the City Council Board meeting on _December 17_.

Social Studies

Standard: Students will understand election processes and responsibilities of citizens.

Objective: The electoral college

Your class has been selected to debate a class at a rival school on the local television station. You must defend the electoral college process. In preparation for your debate, you must research the electoral college, prepare both pro and con arguments, practice debate rules and strategies, and prepare 4" x 6" note cards with key arguments. The debate is scheduled for _February 19_.

Chapter Three

Blackline Masters

Performance Tasks

Subject: _____

Objective: _____

Standards: _____

Task:

Subject: _____

Objective: _____

Standards: _____

Task:

Subject: _____

Objective: _____

Standards: _____

Task:

Subject: _____

Objective: _____

Standards: _____

Task:

SkyLight Professional Development • www.skylightedu.com

Performance Task Plan

Subject:_____ Grade Level_____
Curriculum:_____
Standards:

Performance Task:

Group Work:
      one   two   three   four   five

Individual Work Correlated to Standards:
1.
2.
3.
4.

Methods of Assessment:

Blackline 3.2

Performance Task Checklist

Standard: _____

Assignment: _____

Create a cluster checklist for the Individual Work Assignment in your performance task.

Criteria/Performance Indicators	Not Yet 0	Some Evidence 1
•		
•		
•		
•		
•		
•		
•		
•		
•		
•		
•		
•		
•		
•		
•		
•		
•		
•		
Comments		

Blackline 3.3

SkyLight Professional Development • www.skylightedu.com

Multiple Intelligences Portfolio

Unit:_____ Time Frame:_____ Grade/Subject:_____

Standards: (1) _____

(2) _____

(3) _____

Verbal/ Linguistic	Logical/ Mathematical	Visual/ Spatial	Bodily/ Kinesthetic

Musical/Rhythmic	Interpersonal	Intrapersonal	Naturalist

Standards Pieces	Item 1	Item 2	Item 3	Item 4

Student Choice	Item 5	Item 6	Item 7	Item 8

Blackline 3.4

Chapter 4

Collect
and
Organize

Overview

After defining the purpose of the portfolio and targeting the standards and curriculum goals, the systematic process of developing a portfolio begins. Students start the ongoing process of gathering and collecting artifacts of their work. The process necessitates making decisions about the type of container (notebook, box, bag, envelope, file folder, or photo album), the labeling technique (tabs, table of contents, registry), the order of materials (standards, sequential, thematic), and the overall look of the collection.

These preliminary decisions shape the organization of the portfolio. If order guides portfolio development in the early stages when the number and variety of artifacts is manageable, then order will reign over chaos in the later stages when the amount of material can easily become unmanageable. If order guides this process, students know where to store items. This management phase addresses two concerns: how to collect items for the portfolio and how to organize those items to meet goals.

If order guides portfolio development in the early stages when the number and variety of artifacts is manageable, then order will reign over chaos in the later stages when the amount of material can easily become unmanageable.

Introduction

"A portfolio is a purposeful collection of student work that exhibits the student's efforts, progress, and achievements in one or more areas" (Paulson et al. 1991, p. 60). Most teachers realize that portfolios demonstrate what students know and can do. They also believe portfolios complement paper-and-pencil tests as tools to measure academic skills and make informed instructional decisions. Their concern, however, usually focuses on logistics: How is it possible to collect all the "stuff" from all of my students, organize it into a portfolio system, and still maintain my sanity?

Portfolios take more time and require more planning than assigning work sheets, chapter questions, or homework. Meaningful portfolio projects do not just happen. Portfolios place additional demands on teachers and students and often stretch resources. Teachers, administrators, policymakers, and students find the process of developing a meaningful portfolio challenging and time consuming. Even though teachers welcome the challenge, requiring 150

Here, Mommy

freshmen to keep a portfolio requires courage and planning. Most freshmen collect "stuff"—just look at their bedroom closets or school lockers—but they have trouble organizing their stuff. Teachers who develop a plan at the beginning of the process to handle the logistics of an undertaking of this magnitude enjoy more success. The following options for storage, organizational flow, and organizational tools need to be considered in developing a portfolio plan. (You may use Blackline 4.1 at the end of this chapter to plan the storage, organizational flow, and organizational tools you will use in your portfolio.)

Storage

Hanging Files—Hang It Up

Teachers set up hanging files for each student to serve as a working portfolio that contains all the students' work. Students keep all of their work in the hanging files stored in a file cabinet, milk crate, or box. Plastic milk crates make

excellent portable portfolio systems if file cabinets are not available
or if teachers have to switch classrooms.

Notebooks—Book It

Students in the upper grades keep a three-hole notebook with separate dividers or pocket folders for pieces of work. The pocket folder
stores artifacts, cassettes, or videos. Plastic protectors hold rough
drafts as well as final copies. Drafts and final copies show growth
and provide ways to measure improvement over time.

Rainbow Collection—Rainbowing

Students separate their work into colored folders according to subject
areas, works in progress, best work, "not yet" work, group work, or
integrated assignments. These folders are stored in file cabinets, student desks, or student notebooks. Colored folders help organize a
standards-based portfolio system by designating different subject
areas. The colored folders could also designate standards that have
been exceeded, standards that have been met, and standards that still
need to be met.

Red = Language Arts
Blue = Math
Yellow = Science
Green = Social Studies

Folders—Accordion Pleats

Large folders with accordion pleats can contain big samples, artifacts,
or projects. These could also hold cassette tapes, art, videos, computer disks, file folders, notebooks, and bigger group projects that
require more space than a file folder or binder can provide.

Cereal Boxes—Snap, Crackle, Pop

Elementary teachers like using large cereal boxes to hold student work. They write the student's name on the side panel and store the boxes upright on a shelf like books. The students decorate the front and back of the boxes with artwork or collages. The box then serves as a working portfolio before items are selected to achieve the stated purpose or to meet goals for the final portfolio.

Media Center—Bank Vault

Class or schoolwide portfolios, integrated portfolios, or multiyear portfolios can be placed in accordion-pleated folders and stored in the media center for easy access and review. Students check out their portfolios as needed, especially for updates of the registry, revisions, and conferences to monitor their growth and development over time.

Photo Albums—Snapshots

Photo albums showcase pictures of student projects, group skits, performances, field trips, travels, extracurricular activities, commendations, awards, hobbies, programs from school concerts or plays, articles from school or local newspapers, invitations to events, and ticket stubs from sporting or cultural events. These artifacts provide insight into a student's life, both inside and outside of school. The album portrays the "whole" student through the integration of academic, extracurricular, and social activities.

Computer Disks—Disk It

Students include written work, problem-solving logs, journals, and scripts on computer disks that become a flexible portfolio system. Technology makes it possible to scan pictures, record voices, and use digital pictures. Some schools also include contents of the cumulative folder such as test scores, emergency phone numbers, medical information, and special education individual evaluation programs on the computer disk. The accessibility of the contents of a digital portfolio that contains items from the student's cumulative folder must be monitored carefully for security and confidentiality. See the Examples page for samples of storage systems at the end of this chapter.

Organizational Flow

Although a comprehensive portfolio incorporates many steps, three essential steps—collect, select, reflect—remain crucial to the portfolio's organizational flow (see Figure 4.1). Students collect items, select key items to meet goals, and reflect on the importance of the items in relationship to their goals.

Working Portfolio—Collectibles

After students collect work and store it in an appropriate container, the process is only one-third completed. The collection process takes ten weeks, a quarter, a semester, or a year, depending on the time frame of each class. Many items involve student choice, whereas other items involve teacher selections focused on accountability. After the collection stage, students move to the selection stage. Figure 4.2 lists what students might collect.

Organizational Flow for a Portfolio System

Collect
everything into the
working portfolio

Select
pieces that meet goals
or standards

Reflect
on your selections

Figure 4.1

Final Portfolio—Selectables

The selection process is critical to the portfolio process. The old adage "less is more" is appropriate for the size of a final portfolio. If it is a standards portfolio, only items correlated to meeting the standards are included. The selection process is determined by the purpose of the portfolio, the portfolio's audience, and the type of portfolio. Items can be selected by categories. For example, students select two writing samples, one group project, one performance, one extracurricular entry, one best work, etc. Later in the portfolio process, students refine and reflect upon their selections.

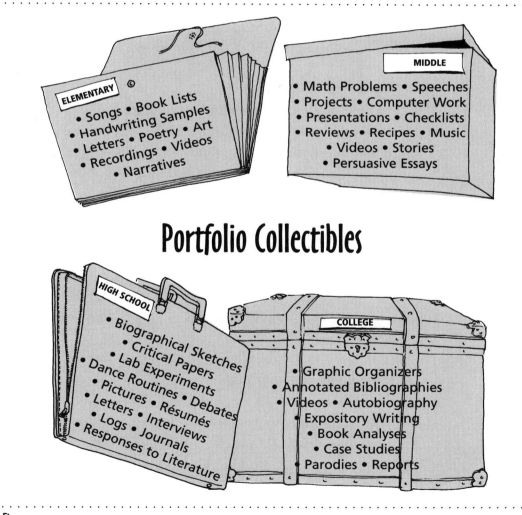

Figure 4.2

Final Portfolio—Reflectibles

Even though teachers require certain entries to be included in the portfolios, students also select entries to be included. In the reflection process, students describe their selections and reflect on what they have learned. See the Examples page at the end of this chapter for a sample organizational flow. You may use Blackline 4.2 (at the end of this chapter) to help determine the sequence of the reflection process.

Organizational Tools

The portfolio's physical set up helps the student and the audience understand the pieces. Organizational tools must be used to make the portfolio user-friendly for the student and other interested parties.

Dividers—Tabs and Dabs

Divided notebook folders or plastic divider pages separate work by genre or subject area, rough drafts and final drafts, best work and "not yet" work, individual work or group work. Dividers also separate the portfolio according to the table of contents. Tabs allow students and their audiences quick access to specific pieces.

Colored Dots—Dotted Swiss

Colored dots in all sizes code entries in the portfolio. The dots help with organization. A code for the dots needs to be included in the table of contents. The coding helps students recognize what still needs to be completed or what still needs to be improved. See Figure 4.3 for a sample code.

Table of Contents—Table It

A table of contents lists all of the entries and corresponding page numbers. Most final portfolios contain between seven and ten items. Approximately seven items represent student work related to the content or standards. Entries like a reflection page, a student self-assessment, and a goal-setting page complete the final portfolio by incorporating thoughtful insight into the student's academic strengths and learning challenges.

SkyLight Professional Development

Colored Dot Codes

Yellow dot	=	First draft
Green dot	=	Second draft
Red dot	=	Final draft
Blue dot	=	Reflection
Black dot	=	Meets standard

Figure 4.3

Artifact Registry—Hotel Registry

Portfolio registries chronicle when and why students remove items (eject) and replace them with newer items (inject) (Dietz 1992). Students record the dates, items, and reasons for the replacement. This ongoing process reinforces students' metacognition—students are thinking about their own thinking and learning processes. A sample of a completed artifact registry appears at the end of this chapter (a blank artifact registry is also provided in Blackline 4.3).

Self-Assessment Stems—Self-Checks

Students empowered to self-assess their knowledge, their progress, and their mastery of the standards develop into independent and self-sufficient learners. Students able to assess their own work based upon predetermined criteria and indicators become more critical thinkers. Rubrics based upon key criteria determine the degree to which students succeed. The dated rubrics used throughout the year allow all stakeholders to review a student's progress and helps determine additional academic goals.

Digital Connection

Students using the artifact registry for digital portfolios can efficiently enter anecdotal records and dates on the entries which they reflect upon and select for continued inclusion in the portfolio.

Biography of a Work Log—Bed to Bed

Wolf (1989) says that long-term projects require "moment-to-moment monitoring, Monday morning quarterbacking, and countless judgments of errors and worth" (p. 35). A biography of a work traces the development of a major project or performance. The biography lists dated entries and chronicles the development of an idea from its inception to the final product or performance; metaphorically, getting up in the morning to going to bed in the evening. The biography of a work log attached to the final product helps the student recognize the entry point or diagnostic benchmark and the progress he or she made toward achieving an academic goal. A sample appears on the Examples page at the end of this chapter. Blackline 4.4 (at the end of this chapter) can be used with students when creating a biography of a work log.

Index—Let Your Fingers Do the Walking

Students compile an alphabetical index of major items at the end of their portfolios. An index serves as an easy reference for specific examples that show evidence of writing skills, multiple intelligences, group work, artwork, extracurricular activities, content, or standards.

Sticky Notes—Note Post

Students want feedback on their work. Formal feedback includes a portfolio evaluation form or scoring rubric; informal feedback includes comments written on sticky notes. Using removable notes means that the students' original work is not violated and grades or comments are removable. The students can review notes and then remove them before sharing the portfolio formally with parents, peers, or visitors during an exhibition.

Portfolio Entry Sheets—Entry Captions

A working portfolio could possibly degenerate into a mess of materials and papers that makes it difficult and time consuming to organize

Sample Portfolio Entry Sheet

Name of Student: _Michael_

Date of Entry: _5/18_

Title or Description of Entry: _Narrative Paper on Most Embarrassing Moment_

Standard Addressed: _Writing Standard E-2_

Why This Entry Is Important: _I think it is humorous and I worked hard on keeping my verb tense consistent and keeping the reader's interest._

Personal Reflection: _I spent a lot of time on this paper because I knew I had to read it to the class. I enjoyed writing this because it made my friends laugh._

Figure 4.4

into a final portfolio. Nitko (2001) suggests attaching a portfolio entry sheet to each item that includes the information needed to identify the item. See Figure 4.4 for a sample. You may use Blackline 4.5 (at the end of this chapter) to create your own portfolio entry sheets.

These tools help all students organize and chronicle their work. Teachers who develop a logical, organizational system to help students take control of their portfolio find the entire process more manageable and more meaningful.

Examples: Collect and Organize

Storage

Organizational Flow

Working Portfolio
(hanging file, notebook, cereal box)

↓

Collect Everything
(five to seven weeks)

↓

Final Portfolios
(folder, computer disk, photo album)

↓

Select Seven to Ten Items
(one or two weeks)

↓

Reflect on Work
(one week)

↓

Hold Conferences
(one week)

Organizational Tool

ARTIFACT REGISTRY

Name *Mary S.*   **Class** *American Literature*

DELETIONS

Date	Item	Reasons for Deleting
4/18/01	Book report on *The Great Gatsby*	I didn't understand symbolism so I used Cliff Notes. Not my best work.
4/30/01	Sonnet on Sylvia Plath	I was so worried about a rhyme scheme that content suffered.

ADDITIONS

Date	Item	Reasons for Adding
4/18/01	Book report on *Tender Is the Night*	I liked this book by Fitzgerald better. I could figure out symbolism on my own.
4/30/01	Free verse poem on Plath	It didn't rhyme, but I said what I felt. More meaningful.

Organizational Tool

BIOGRAPHY OF A WORK LOG

Assignment: *Present a Decade in History*

Date	Log Entry
5/2/01	Group voted to pick the decade of the 1920s for presentation.
5/3/01	Brainstormed ideas for key elements of decade.
5/7/01	Went to media center to research key elements.
5/8/01	Divided key elements among 5 members: (1) historical events (4) music (2) politics (5) art (3) clothes
5/9–5/16/01	Gathered information, costumes, music, artifacts, newspaper headlines.
5/17–5/23/01	Wrote script for skit, made slides, selected music.
5/24/01	Presented retrospect of 1920s to the class.

Comments: The group worked well together. We learned the Charleston!

Chapter Four

Blackline Masters

Teacher Planner
Portfolio Collection and Organization

Storage
How and where will I **store** my portfolios?

. . . .

. . . .

. . . .

Organizational Flow
What is my **time line** for collecting, selecting, reflecting, and conferencing?

. . . .

. . . .

. . . .

Organizational Tools
What types of **tools** (table of contents, tabs, index) will I use to organize the portfolios?

. . . .

. . . .

. . . .

Questions
What **questions** do I have about the collection process?

. . . .

. . . .

. . . .

Security
How will I ensure the **confidentiality** of the portfolios?

. . . .

. . . .

. . . .

SkyLight Professional Development • www.skylightedu.com

Portfolio Organizational Flow

Collect Items for Working Portfolios

Dates:_____

Select Items for Final Portfolio

Dates:_____

Describe and Reflect on All Items

Dates:_____

Conference with Peers and Teacher

Dates:_____

Blackline 4.2

Artifact Registry

Student_____ **Class**_____

DELETIONS

Date	Item	Reasons for Deleting

ADDITIONS

Date	Item	Reasons for Adding

SkyLight Professional Development • www.skylightedu.com

Biography of a Work Log

Assignment:_____

Standard:_____

Date	Log Entry

Comments:

Signed:_____

Date:_____

Blackline 4.4

Portfolio Entry

Standard:

Title or Description of Entry: _____
_____
_____

Personal Reflection: _____
_____
_____
_____

Student:_____ Grade:_____ Date:_____

- -

Portfolio Entry

Standard:

Title or Description of Entry: _____
_____
_____

Personal Reflection: _____
_____
_____
_____

Student:_____ Grade:_____ Date:_____

SkyLight Professional Development • www.skylightedu.com

Select Key Artifacts

Overview

Many students become pack rats, accumulating large masses of papers and projects in a portfolio if teachers do not focus on the selection process. Often, teachers believe the collection process *is* the final portfolio. They forget the second important step—selection—which is when students prune the items in order to arrive at a final product. The selection process links the portfolio more specifically to the purpose. If the purpose of the portfolio is to meet standards, then artifacts need to be selected to meet the standards. Representative pieces for each type of work need to be included. In a writing portfolio, narratives, expository pieces, business letters, and journal entries as well as literary critiques should link directly to each standard. The purpose of the portfolio determines what items to select for the final or showcase portfolio.

Criteria for evaluation is formalized. Teachers decide if general guidelines or more specific criteria are appropriate. Decisions about who selects the artifacts and when the selections are made must be determined. In any case, the selection process focuses on determining what entries need to be culled from a working portfolio and included in the final portfolio.

SELECTION PROCESS QUESTIONS:
- What is the purpose of the portfolio?
- What is the criteria for artifact selection?
- Who selects artifacts?
- When are artifacts selected?

The selection process links the portfolio to the purpose. The purpose of the portfolio determines what items to select for the final or showcase portfolio.

Introduction

"When you and your students are clear about the criteria for selecting entries at the beginning of the portfolio process, the process tends to result in a fair, focused, and efficient assessment" (Rolheiser et al. 2000 p. 17). Since the portfolio selection process correlates so closely with the purpose and type of the portfolio, only the items that achieve that purpose are included. For example, an employability portfolio contains evidence of a student's potential in the work force. Lists of courses in a particular field, recommendations, a résumé, examples of work, and previous job experience support the student's candidacy for a specific position. The types of portfolios described in chapter one dictate the selection of specific items that demonstrate the person's understanding or expertise in a particular area.

The selection process, therefore, begins with several important questions about portfolios:

- What should be included?
- How will the items be selected?
- Who will select the items?
- When will these items be selected?

What Should Be Included?

The focus may be on particular subject matter, various learning processes, the spectrum of multiple intelligences, a special project or unit, or standards. The portfolio could also be designed around a particular unit of study, concept, or theme.

Subject or Content Area Learning—Just the Facts

Items that demonstrate what a student understands about a particular subject area, such as language arts, mathematics, science, or art, would be included in a subject or content area portfolio. Students and teachers work together to select the types of items that are representative of important concepts and skills in each subject area. A portfolio for a language arts class, for example, could contain:

- book reports,
- key vocabulary words,
- a research paper,
- a response journal to a piece of literature,
- a letter to the editor,
- a poem,
- a panel discussion,
- a performance tape of a scene from a play,
- a reflection on the portfolio,
- a self-assessment, and
- a list of future goals.

The students and the teacher would decide upon the guidelines and criteria for selecting items to include.

Digital Connection

Digital portfolios complement the decision-making portfolio process. Students engaged in electronic portfolio development continually apply and develop proficiency in the application of technology and telecommunication tools to their portfolios. In addition, entries are organized, searchable, and readily available. This makes the selection process much easier.

Learning Process—The Experience

In this type of portfolio, teachers and students select items that represent the learning process. The content becomes a means to achieve an end. The portfolio focuses on the students' skills and processes like speaking, listening, writing, reading, problem solving, decision making, or higher-order thinking. The students' proficiencies in these areas are demonstrated through written work, cassettes and videos of oral work, teacher observations checklists, and interviews and conferences with students. A sample matrix for a learning process portfolio is shown on the Examples page at the end of this chapter. A matrix to use with your students can be found on Blackline 5.1 at the end of this chaper.

Multiple Intelligences—The Spectrum

A multiple intelligences portfolio showcases entries that represent all eight intelligences of the student. The student might include:

- logs and journals to depict verbal/linguistic and intrapersonal intelligences;
- a Venn diagram to depict visual/spatial intelligence;
- a computer program to depict logical/mathematical intelligence;
- a video of a group performance to depict bodily/kinesthetic and interpersonal intelligences;
- a rap song to represent musical/rhythmic intelligence; and
- a nature walk analysis to represent naturalist intelligence.

Students select items that showcase their talents and explain why they feel they are strong in some areas and need work in others. Not only does this type of portfolio require a wide variety of entries, but it also stretches students to expand their repertoire of products and processes to meet academic goals.

Standards-Based—High Stakes

In a standards-based portfolio, all artifacts correlate to specific performance and content standards. Each entry has a standard listed on the top. Students sometimes fill out an entry sheet to describe the standard and complete a checklist or rubric to indicate academic achievement in each area. The dated entries show developmental growth over time.

Thematic Units or Projects—Dream Theme

The unit or thematic portfolio has always been popular. Instead of including items from the entire quarter or semester, the portfolio is focused on a specific unit of study. The unit ranges from two to five weeks in length and the portfolio contains ten to twelve items. If the students study Greek mythology for five weeks, they select entries that demonstrate their writing, reading, and speaking processes and their understanding of Greek myths, history, and customs. For example, a thematic portfolio on mythology might include a poem about the first football game on Mt. Olympus, a modern version of the Twelve Labors of Hercules, a Venn diagram comparing the Greeks and the Trojans, a myth explaining the origin of fireflies, a video of Olympic events, and drawings of products derived from Greek names. The teacher may require some categories that meet curriculum goals or standards, but the students often have a choice about the specific entries. (See the Appendix for a sample portfolio on mythology.)

How Will the Items Be Selected?

In conjunction with determining what goes into the portfolio, attention must be paid to how the entries are selected. Do the entries demonstrate a student's ability to meet learning goals and state standards? Sometimes the criteria and indicators for quality work are established by the teacher and the students in the classroom. Other times, many of these high-stakes assignments require the use of rubrics created by the district and state to ensure reliability and validity. (Rubrics are discussed in detail in chapter eight.) See Blackline 5.2 for a graphic organizer which lists all the possible selections for a final portfolio.

National Standards—Think Globally

During the past decade groups representing subject area professional associations, national accreditation organizations, and child advocacy organizations created national standards. Each standard incorporates emergent knowledge in education as well as the best educational practices. Teachers often find these national standards to be an excellent source for determining local school or classroom standards and criteria for student achievement.

State Mandates—State's Stakes

State standards correlated to state tests and curriculum frameworks also determine criteria for selecting portfolio artifacts. In many instances, students and teachers work together to translate state standards in subject areas or learning processes into student-friendly criteria for performances. Teachers create student self-assessment forms and artifact selection forms. In this way, the portfolio selection process assures that content, goals, and artifacts reflect clearly defined criteria that meet standards and benchmarks and also help students perform on state standardized tests. For a sample of a plan for meeting state standards, see the Examples page at the end of this chapter. For a form to use with your students, see Blackline 5.3 at the end of this chapter.

District Goals—Act Locally

Teachers are also required to implement district-mandated standards across the curriculum and develop criteria in key areas to determine the selection of portfolio artifacts. Standards that delineate criteria and indicators of performance will result in portfolios that reflect acceptable and outstanding levels of accomplishment at each level of student achievement.

Teacher- and Student-Created Criteria—It's Up to Us!

If the purpose of the portfolio is to review student work and set new goals, then the teacher and students develop the selection process. For example, the class votes to include representative work, but the

Selection Categories

Media
cassettes
slides
videos
pictures
computer programs

Group Work
projects
performances
peer reviews
peer edits
social skills

Individual Work
papers
tests
journals
logs
homework

Processes
biographies of works
rough drafts and
    final drafts
sketches and final
    drawings
problem-solving
    attempts

Reflective
self-assessments
reflections
reflective journals
artifact registries
goal setting logs
learning log

Multiple Intelligences
logical/mathematical
musical/rhythmic
verbal/linguistic
bodily/kinesthetic
visual/spatial
interpersonal
intrapersonal
naturalist

Figure 5.1

students have some choice as to which items they include. They also create their own rubrics to assess the items according to criteria and indicators they determine. To help inform the selection process, see Figure 5.1 for a list of selection categories

Who Will Select the Items?

Who are the stakeholders in the portfolio process? Who will participate in the selection of artifacts? Once again, the purpose of the portfolio determines who will select the items. Following is an outline of a number of combinations of the decision makers that may be involved in the process.

District- or State-Mandated Artifacts—It's the Law

If the portfolio is part of the formal assessment process to monitor student achievement and teacher accountability, district or state educational leaders mandate which entries must be included. For example, a state might require one biographical piece, a piece of creative writing, a résumé for a job, evidence of teamwork, an assignment that integrates two different subject areas, a problem and a solution, or a self-assessment. Some state departments of education determine what pieces will be selected for high-stakes portfolios that often play a big role in the evaluation process. The state usually provides a scoring guide or rubric to help teachers and students know the expectations of quality work and to compare students' work to the standards. The portfolio may be used in conjunction with grades, standardized test scores, and teacher recommendations to determine promotion or retention of students.

Student-Selected Artifacts—It's Up to Me!

Some teachers allow students to select all of the work they want to include in their portfolios. They recognize that students comprise the major stakeholders in the process and, therefore, should be responsible for their own learning. Some students select only their best work; others include a few works in progress, unsatisfactory pieces, and "not yets." Others highlight their lives outside of school and choose to select extracurricular, hobby, job-related, or community projects that reveal the whole student. Wiggins (1994) stresses that the selection process should be thoughtful and fun—but also challenging.

Teacher-Selected Artifacts—I Have Goals

The teacher plays a critical role in the selection of portfolio pieces. The teacher's input ranges from obvious to subtle. The teacher makes choices to ensure the items reflect school, district, or state requirements. These so-called high-stakes portfolios require certain entries. At other times, the teacher exercises the option to include any pieces that reflect the content or processes that represent the key concepts in the course. Teachers mix student-generated work with their own observations, quarterly or semester progress reports, scores on important standardized tests or teacher-made tests, anecdotal records, absentee records, or other items included in the student's cumulative records. In this case, the confidentiality of the portfolio is paramount. These types of entries limit the access of portfolios because peers and other teachers will violate confidentiality issues by reviewing them.

Teacher-/Student-Selected Artifacts—Together Is Better

The teacher and student select artifacts that they both agree best meet the standards and criteria. Teachers plan for teacher/student selections to occur at natural intersections of teaching and learning, such as the completion of thematic units of study or at the end of the quarter. Often the teacher decides to include three or four items to meet content goals or district goals and then allows students free choice on the rest of the selections.

Additionally, teachers assign categories—creative writing pieces, group projects, artwork, performances, media projects, reflections, logs, journals, a self-check observation list—but allow students the freedom to review their work and select their best entries in each category. This process allows the teacher to retain evidence of growth or achievement related to curriculum goals and standards while at the same time allowing students to retain their freedom of choice within the teacher's prescribed framework.

Peer-Selected Artifacts—All for One, One for All

Peer-selected artifacts involve the classroom community. Students intricately involved in the assessment process review the work of other students, offer constructive feedback, and help select pieces to include in another student's portfolio. For example, one student may feel a piece of artwork is not up to his usual standards and would rather not include it in his portfolio. A fellow student or the members of his group, however, may recognize qualities in the piece that make it worthy of entry into the portfolio. The peer requests that the student include the entry and attaches a commentary or reflection describing why the peer thinks the work is important.

Students in the peer selection process listen empathetically, use encouraging words, and disagree with the idea—not the person. They assess the quality of work based on standards, criteria, and indicators included in the rubrics. The involvement of peers in the selection process encourages team building, trust building, and cooperation within the classroom community.

Parent- and/or Significant Other-Selected Artifacts—Tell Me What You Think

Parents and other significant persons, such as caregivers or guardians, other teachers, counselors, siblings, principals, and bus drivers, play a vital role in the selection process. Students ask parents or others to review and select entries to include in their portfolios. This procedure helps parents become a part of the learning process and encourages students to discuss work with other people, not just the teacher. Parents can monitor students' progress throughout the quarter instead of just at the end. For a sample of a parent selection, see the Examples page at the end of this chapter.

Teachers can provide parents or significant others with key questions to ask when making their selections. The parents or significant others write a reflection piece or commentary stating what they liked about the entry and why they thought it should or should not be included in the student's portfolio.

When Will These Items Be Selected?

The what, how, and who aspects of the selection process are important. Another dimension to be considered is the when. Common occasions to make final selections for the portfolio are parent conferences, the end of a thematic unit, the end of a quarter or a semester, and the end of the year. Another option is to create a cumulative portfolio with work within a chosen time span.

Parent Conferences—Parent Talk

Portfolio reviews held during parent conferences provide valuable feedback for students, parents, and teachers. These portfolio conferences could take place during the end of any quarter or semester or at the end-of-year evaluation. The portfolio provides more concrete data than a grade book for communicating learner outcomes, student achievements, and student goals. Once again, parents review student work to ascertain their students' understanding of key concepts and attainment of important skills.

End of Thematic Unit—The End

Whenever the students finish a unit on a content area topic, a book, a period of history, a learning process, or an integrated unit, they share their collected artifacts. The finished portfolio is more than just a notebook of stuff—it is a memento of the unit that students value because their own creativity and thought went into the final product.

End of Quarter/Semester—Seasons

Portfolio selection and sharing aligns with the traditional end-of-term reporting procedures that commonly occur in schools. If portfolios are reviewed on a quarterly or semester basis, students and parents review previous goals and reflect on work in progress. Teachers reflect on student progress, assemble anecdotal notes and checklists, and assist students in making artifact selections that represent achievement of ongoing goals, attainment of standards, and mastery of critical learning processes.

> The portfolio provides more concrete data than a grade book for communicating learner outcomes, student achievements, and student goals.

End of Year—It's a Wrap!

The end of the year portfolio provides the final opportunity for students, teachers, and parents to select artifacts that represent the key learning experiences and learning outcomes that students have achieved. These portfolios are shared during classroom or schoolwide exhibitions where parents, family, community members, and other educators review student portfolios and interview students about their learning. The selection of this final portfolio usually represents key learnings, important concepts, big questions, thematic units, and other representative work from the whole year. It may also be used for promotion or retention if districts use multiple measures of assessment to determine passing grades. In some states, students who fail high-stakes state tests may submit a portfolio and the teacher's recommendation to support the student's promotion to the next grade.

Cumulative—Year-to-Year

Schools may maintain cumulative portfolios that are passed on to each grade for several years or for the entire school period of K–12. The cumulative portfolio is usually designed to include satisfactory and exemplary student achievements of performance standards throughout several years of each student's school career.

Either the teacher or the school determines the checkpoints at which students select or review portfolio contents to provide evidence of their achievements. Depending on the purposes of portfolios, the cumulative portfolio provides a platform to report student achievement of school goals and standards. Periodically, a review and audit of the portfolio takes place to remove some items before adding

The Portfolio Selection Process

"I kept saying, 'Maybe we should clean off the front of the refrigerator,' but noooo . . ."

SkyLight Professional Development

new ones—no school could possibly store all the portfolios for a long period of time. Computer disks provide another option.

The timing of the selection process depends on the purpose, the type, the school schedule, conference dates, and other logistics that make the whole portfolio process valuable as well as workable. It is important to establish the dates of the checkpoints throughout the year in order to assure regular monitoring and to allow sufficient time for students to review, reflect, and self-assess their own portfolios during the selection process. For a sample calendar of checkpoints throughout the year, see the Examples page at the end of this chapter.

The selection process may seem daunting. It can be difficult for students to choose objectively and even subjectively from a seemingly vast amount of work. If students and teachers take the time to plan for selection, choosing carefully from the options presented in Figure 5.2, the process will be a more enjoyable task. For forms to help in the selection process, see Blacklines 5.3–5.6 at the end of this chapter.

Portfolio Selection Process Options

What to Include in the Portfolio? (Purpose)

- ❏ Subject or Content Area
- ❏ Multiple Intelligences
- ❏ Learning Processes
- ❏ Standards-Based
- ❏ Thematic Units or Projects

How to Select Items? (Criteria)

- ❏ National Standards
- ❏ Teacher- and Student-Created Criteria
- ❏ State Mandates
- ❏ District Goals

Who Selects Items?

- ❏ District or State
- ❏ Peers
- ❏ Parents/Significant Others
- ❏ Students
- ❏ Teachers
- ❏ Teacher/Student

When to Select Items?

- ❏ Parent Conferences
- ❏ End of Thematic Unit
- ❏ End of Quarter/Semester
- ❏ End of Year
- ❏ Cumulative (2–3 years)

Figure 5.2

Examples: Select Key Artifacts

The What
PLANNING MATRIX:
LEARNING PROCESS PORTFOLIO

Student: _Brittany_   Date: _11/12_

Assessment Tools	Speaking	Listening Attentively and Empathetically	Writing	Reading	Evaluating – Checking for Accuracy (Applying)	Reasoning	Problem Solving	Questioning/Predicting
Journals	–	–	–	–	–	–	–	–
Audio or Video Samples	+	✓	✓	+	+	✓	✓	+
Teacher/Peer Checklist	+	+	✓	✓	+	+	+	+
Interviews	+	+	✓	✓	+	✓	✓	✓
Extended Projects	✓	✓	✓	✓	✓	✓	✓	✓

✓ at least one artifact
✚ two or more artifacts
– ongoing piece

The How

Select items for the portfolio that meet state goals in science.

Student: _Matt_   Grade/Class: _8_   Date: _3/15_

Standards	Portfolio Entry	Date Completed
Know basic vocabulary of biological science	Vocabulary test	10/3
Know implications and limitations of technical development	Book report on *Brave New World*	11/15
Know principles of scientific research	Journal entry	1/22
Know processes of science	Lab report on experiment	2/9

The Who
PARENT SELECTION

To: Parent/Significant Other

Please review the attached entries that may be included in _Jim R.'s_ portfolio and provide your feedback.

What piece most surprises you? Why?
The cartoon! I had no idea Jim could draw that well and think of such a clever caption.

Which piece do you feel needs more work? Why?
The job application. It makes me cringe when I see spelling and grammar errors.

Which piece do you want to include in the portfolio? Why?
The report on health care reform. Jim did a lot of research for that one.

Signature _Mr. John Ross_

The When
PORTFOLIO SCHEDULE FOR THE YEAR

October 5	Portfolio review by parents at back-to-school night
November 3	12-week review by: Peer Teacher
February 5	12-week review by: Peer Teacher Students in other class
April 25	12-week review by: Parents/significant other Cooperative group members Teacher
June 5	Final Portfolio Review Teacher and parents

SkyLight Professional Development

Chapter Five

Blackline Masters

Planning Matrix
Learning Process Portfolio

Student: _____ Class: _____ Date: _____

Assessment Tools	Speaking	Listening	Writing	Reading	Checking for Accuracy	Problem-Solving	Questioning	

✓ at least one artifact

✚ two or more artifacts

— ongoing piece

Blackline 5.1

118 THE PORTFOLIO CONNECTION

SkyLight Professional Development • www.skylightedu.com

Possible Selection for Final Portfolio

Use the following chart to organize and plan selections for the final portfolio. The teacher should select the required pieces first and then tell the students to select entries they feel showcase their best work.

Teacher—Standard	**Student Pick—Standard**

Teacher—Standard	**Student Pick—Free Choice**

Teacher—Curriculum Goal	**Student Self-Assessment**

Peer/Parent Pick	**Student Reflection**

Student Pick—Standard	**Student Goal Setting**

Blackline 5.2

Standards Log

List the standards then list the portfolio entries that address each standard.

Student:_____ **Grade/Class:**_____ **Date:**_____

Standards	Portfolio Entry	Date Completed

Blackline 5.3

SkyLight Professional Development • www.skylightedu.com

Teacher Planner
Selecting Key Artifacts

The What

What will be the curricular or learning areas for which student portfolios will be used?

[ ] Subject or Content Area Learning
[ ] Learning Process
[ ] Multiple Intelligences
[ ] Standards-Based
[ ] Thematic Units or Projects
[ ] Other

Comments:

. . . .

. . . .

The How

Standards and Criteria for Portfolios

- How will standards be determined?

- What standards will be used?
    [ ] National Standards
    [ ] State Standards
    [ ] District Goals
    [ ] Teacher- and Student-Created Criteria

Comments:

. . . .

. . . .

(continued on next page)

Blackline 5.4

(Teacher Planner Continued)

The Who
Who will participate in the assessment process and selection of the artifacts?

Choose   Explain

[ ] District- or State-
     Mandated   _____
[ ] Student-Selected   _____
[ ] Teacher-Selected   _____
[ ] Teacher-/Student-Selected   _____
[ ] Peer-Selected   _____
[ ] Parent- and/or Significant
     Other-Selected

Comments:

. . . .

. . . .

The When
When will work be selected for inclusion in the portfolio?

[ ] Parent Conferences   Date: _____
[ ] End of Thematic Unit   Date: _____
[ ] End of Quarter/Semester   Date: _____
[ ] End of Year   Date: _____
[ ] Cumulative (Year-to-Year)   Years: _____

Comments:

. . . .

. . . .

Blackline 5.4 (continued)

SkyLight Professional Development • www.skylightedu.com

Portfolio Selection

Date: _____

To: Parent/Significant Other

Please review the attached entries that may be included in _____
portfolio and provide your feedback.   (student's name)

What piece most surprises you? Why?

Which piece do you feel needs more work? Why?

Which piece do you want to include in the portfolio? Why?

Signature: _____

Date: _____

Blackline 5.5

Portfolio Schedule for the Year

Dates	Event

SkyLight Professional Development • www.skylightedu.com

Inspect to Self-Assess

Overview

In contrast to piece-by-piece metacognitive reflections discussed in the next chapter, the inspect phase reviews the entire collection of works to arrive at a self-assessment of the portfolio by the student. This is an important part of the overall classroom evaluation process as students become partners in evaluating their own work—the heart of the portfolio process. Rolheiser, Bower, and Stevahn (2000) state that "self-evaluation is an important part of metacognition . . . it ocurrs when students make judgments about their achievement and react to judgments" (p. 34). Students must review their collection of artifacts. Students can use this time to match their work with predetermined goals, review overall strengths and weaknesses, make adjustments, and determine future directions.

THE INSPECTION PROCESS:

- an overview of the entire collection of artifacts in the portfolio
- promotes student self-assessment, informal or formal
- promotes review of goals and setting of new goals

In this phase, students review both their short- and long-term goals while checking how the portfolio reflects these goals. Checklists can be created to help students evaluate how well they met their academic goals. These checklists can become precursors to more complex scoring guides called rubrics, which will be discussed in chapter eight. With the checklist, the student simply checks "Yes, I did this," or "No, I did not do this," whereas the rubric requires indicators of the quality of the work. The checklist delineates the overall goals of the portfolio assessment process. More specifically, the checklist references particular standards that have been targeted for the project, as well as technical requirements for the final portfolio itself. See Figure 6.1 for a sample checklist.

The inspecting phase is the time for an informal self-evaluation, a check of the overall direction desired by the student. It is the opportunity to ask questions about the next steps along the chosen or changing pathway. It is the moment of truth that signals to learners whether or not they are on track, what measures they might need to take to realign their aims and goals, or if setting new goals may lead them in an entirely different direction. (See Blackline 6.1 at the end of the chapter for a teacher planner on the selection process.)

Sample Portfolio Inspection Checklist

	YES	NO
Goals		
1. Integrate technology into the biology project.		
2. Learn about a genetic disease.		
3. Demonstrate a personal pedigree.		
Standards		
1. Show evidence of the writing process.		
2. Demonstrate understanding of the concept of inherited traits.		
Requirements		
1. Include ten items in portfolio.		
2. Reflect on each item.		
3. Add a table of contents.		
4. Complete the project on time.		
5. Share my portfolio with a partner.		

Figure 6.1

Introduction

"When teachers invite students to become partners in inquiry, to collaborate with them in wondering about what and how students are learning, schools become more thoughtful places" (Atwell 1991, p. 3). An exciting outcome of using portfolios is the recognition by students that they themselves have become the center of the learning process. This occurs when teachers develop thoughtful goals for their students and get them to think about their learning achievements. Students who are active participants in the portfolio collection and selection process are empowered to become autonomous, independent thinkers, problem solvers, and creators of new knowledge.

Teachers who invite, extend, and commend the learning of their students move more closely toward genuine assessment. In fact, they approach the root meaning of assess—*assidere*—*to sit beside*. Learning is "seen as a joint venture where students and teachers learn together. It then follows that the responsibility for evaluation must also be shared by the teacher and the students" (Howell and Woodley, cited in Goodman et al. 1992, p. 87).

Wiggins (1994) says the aim of educators "should be to make all students able to monitor and reflect on their own work so they can self-adjust" as needed. Students need to take responsibility for inspecting their work for quality. People inspect their own products or performances according to standards and then self-assess, self-adjust, and set new goals on an ongoing basis. Student autonomy has become an emergent goal of education, because "autonomy in the intellectual realm means ability to govern oneself by being able to take relevant factors into account" (Kamii et al. 1994, p. 675).

Goal setting and self-inspection also foster self-initiative. Students become willing to take intellectual risks and to assume both responsibility and accountability for their learning. Rolheiser, Bower, and Stevahn (2000) believe that "providing opportunities for students to set goals can support an upward cycle of learning. Setting goals helps students who have negative orientations toward learning or who do not have realistic views of their strengths and weaknesses" (p. 77). To promote student autonomy, initiative, self-assessment, and goal setting, teachers choose from assessment tools such as checklists, logs, journals, learning lists, stem statements, and rubrics. Self-assessment tools can help students evaluate group and individual work, performances, or products. Assessment tools assist students in achieving responsibility for determining the direction of their learning and blueprints for reaching their goals. Teachers begin the self-assessment process by first establishing criteria and then using checklists.

Establishing Criteria—What Is Important

In the reflective stage, students look at each individual piece in their portfolio and react to it. In the inspection stage, students look at the whole portfolio and reflect on how well the entries show whether they have met the criteria for quality work. The teacher and the

> Assessment tools are most effective when they assist students in achieving ownership and responsibility or a sense of voice in determining the direction of their authentic learning and how their journey will be accomplished.

students list criteria they think are important for meeting goals, outcomes, or local and state standards. For example, criteria for a finished portfolio might include several items that show evidence of thoughtfulness, growth and development, process, understanding, and cooperation. Figure 6.2 lists other possible criteria.

Obviously, teachers and students need to prioritize criteria. Later, they can expand the list as students become more proficient in the portfolio process, or as additional criteria are generated. Examples of how these criteria can be expanded to include specific indicators or characteristics are provided in chapter eight. The next step is to develop a scoring sheet or rubric for more specific feedback and/or to evaluate the portfolio for a grade. Even if the portfolio is not graded, students still need to examine their work using the criteria since this process leads to a more thoughtful inspection of their work.

Criteria for Portfolios

- Accuracy of information
- Completeness
- Connections to other subjects
- Correctness of form
- Creativity
- Deadlines and benchmarks met
- Development of process
- Diversity of entries
- Evidence of multiple intelligences
- Evidence of thoughtfulness

- Growth and development
- Insightfulness
- Knowledge of concepts
- Organization
- Persistence (drafts)
- Progress toward goals
- Quality products
- Self-assessment
- Timelines (due dates)
- Visual appeal

Figure 6.2

Creating Checklists—Checking It Twice

Checklists are often used for observational and anecdotal assessment because they assist students in self-assessment and peer assessment. Students use checklists to evaluate progress in work habits, study skills, and organizational skills. (See Figures 6.3 and 6.4; also see the Examples page and Blackline 6.2 at the end of this chapter.) Students learn how to reflect on intelligent behaviors such as persistence, checking for accuracy, and insightfulness (Costa 1991).

Teachers sometimes feel they must observe students and use checklists. For students to become self-regulating, however, they need to monitor their own behavior, products, work habits, thinking skills, and the behavior and products of their peers. Checklists provide concrete information that can be discussed in conferences when students set their new goals. Students review group behavior by checking off when they or their peers demonstrate positive social skills. They can review the checklist and reflect on successes or areas that need improvement. Teachers, students, and group members utilize checklists to inspect learning skills, social skills, or behaviors and set new goals.

Self-Assessment Checklist

Student: _Juanita_   Date: _10/12_

Criterion—Persistence	Not Yet	Seldom	Sometimes	Most of the time
Indicators:				
1. I know how to access information.	✓			
2. I try several approaches.		✓		
3. I do not give up quickly.		✓		
4. I have patience.				✓
5. I brainstorm alternative solutions.	✓			
6. I check my own work.		✓		
7. I write several drafts.		✓		
8. I problem solve.			✓	

Figure 6.3

SkyLight Professional Development

Criteria Checklist

Name: _Kim J._   Grade: _1_

Reading Standard: Apply reading strategies to improve understanding and fluency.

Benchmarks:
- Establish purpose for reading.
- Identify genres.
- Check for understanding.
- Read age-appropriate material.

	NOT YET 0	SOMETIMES 1
Purpose for Reading		
Make predictions.	✓	
Connect key ideas.		✓
Link text to prior knowledge.		✓
Identify Genres		
Fiction		✓
Nonfiction	✓	
Poetry		✓
Check for Understanding		
Reread text.		✓
Read ahead.		✓
Use visual and context clues.	✓	
Ask questions.	✓	
Read Alouds		
Loudness		✓
Fluency		✓
Accuracy of pronunciation		✓

Figure 6.4

Self-Inspection—Inspect, Reflect

Once students begin to self-monitor with checklists, it is time to guide them to not only inspect the work in their portfolios but to also take time to reflect on what they have learned and what portfolio pieces to polish. Logs, learning lists, reflective journals, pictorial lists, and analyses of strenghs and challenges are the most appropriate tools for reflective inspection. This process helps students know if they are on track to meet standards and can be used as a catalyst for new goal setting.

Learning Logs—Log Your Reflections

Learning logs promote student self-reflection. "Logs usually consist of short, more objective entries that contain mathematics, problem-solving entries, observations of science experiments, questions about the lecture or reading, lists of outside readings, homework assignments, or anything that lends itself to keeping records" (Burke 1993, p. 84). Logs provide succinct record keeping.

Learning Lists—First, Second, Third . . .

Learning lists include stem statements that trigger students' thinking about attributes or objectives within the learning process. Learning lists enable students to think backward about their achievements, acknowledge or celebrate them, and record them in a sequential way (see Figure 6.5). (For a form to use with students, see Blackline 6.3 at the end of this chapter.) Sometimes teachers interview each student about revisions or additions to learning lists. Various stem statements trigger students to list what they have learned. Stem statements include *New things I have learned . . . ; One thing I'm having trouble with . . . ;* or *Stories I have written.* Learning lists help students focus on their learning by writing what they have learned and by thinking about items that are difficult for them.

LEARNING LISTS:

- enable students to think about their achievements
- allow students to acknowledge or celebrate their achievements
- help students record achievements in a sequential way

My Learning Lists

Name **Mindy**   Grade **8th   Mythology Unit**

Vocabulary terms and allusions I have learned:

He is an <u>Adonis.</u>   a <u>herculean</u> task   a <u>hydra</u>-headed woman

a <u>titanic</u> problem   the <u>Midas</u> touch   <u>Medusa</u>-haired woman

<u>Pandora's</u> box   He worked like a <u>Trojan.</u>   <u>Cassandra</u> warning

---

Stories and books I have read:

"The Twelve Labors of Hercules"

The Iliad

The Odyssey

"Pandora's Box"

Stories and poems I have written:

"The First Super Bowl on Mt. Olympus"

"The Modern-Day Labors of Hercules"

"Original Myth to Explain How We Got Lightning Bugs"

Things I am having trouble with:

Working a video camera

Understanding Pythagorean Theorem

Working with a group

Important things I have learned:

How pride (hubris) and jealousy can be the downfall of all men and women

How many words come from Greek mythology

Figure 6.5

Reflective Journals—Mirror, Mirror . . .

Reflective journals engage students in ongoing goal setting and reflections and foster the development of interpersonal skills. Unlike logs, which are objective and factual, journals provide students with an ongoing diary of their daily responses, their own subjective feelings, or their narrative viewpoint. Goals set by students are continuously monitored and reflected upon in a reflective journal.

Double-Entry Journals—Double Dip

Double-entry journals enable students to record initial experiences in one column and to respond to or reflect on these experiences in a second column. This format helps students formulate initial observations about a subject in one column, then wait until they have learned more about the topic through time, course work, readings, and videos before they complete the second column. Students recognize how they often change their feelings based upon new experiences. When students use their journals to inspect portfolios, students write about their initial feelings about preparing a portfolio and then reflect many weeks later after they complete their portfolio. A sample of a double-entry journal is provided on the Examples page at the end of this chapter. (For a form to use with students, see Blackline 6.4 at the end of this chapter.)

Dialogue Journals—He Said, She Said

Dialogue journals can take the form of learning logs, reflective journals, or double-entry journals. But dialogue journals are also read by the teacher or others. Dialogue journal promote the development of a student's "voice." They also allow the teacher to enter into the reflection process with each learner. Teachers can write responses directly into the student journal or attach brief notes to the pages. The dialogue journal can be utilized throughout the portfolio or saved until the whole portfolio is complete. This type of feedback provides an outside viewpoint that questions, compliments, and often validates what the student is feeling about his or her work. Constructive feedback of this kind is critical to the portfolio process.

Digital Connection

As more schools promote Web-based or engaged learning curricula, it is possible to provide evidence of a team's achievement of learning outcomes through the digital portfolio. The application of technology allows each student to contribute to a team portfolio that clearly shows each member's unique contribution toward achievement of the lesson or unit objectives.

Pictorial Lists—Draw-a-Long

Pictorial lists are an adaptation of learning lists. Younger children can use the pictorial list to draw pictures. Older students can use a class camera to capture moments of learning that they value, attach pictures to a response sheet, and write their reasons for valuing the activity (Burke 1991).

Analysis of Strengths and Challenges—Have and Have Nots

If students are to develop the critical thinking skills of analysis, synthesis, and evaluation, they need to review their own work and analyze their strengths and their challenges or their "not yets." It is important that students analyze their attributes through several lenses of content, processes, and social skills. Well-rounded students demonstrate competence in all areas or are at least aware of areas that need improvement. See Figure 6.6 and the Examples page (at the end of this chapter) for samples. (For a form to use with students, see Blackline 6.5 at the end of this chapter.)

Setting Goals—The Long and Short of It

As students inspect their portfolios, they analyze and evaluate their goals and plans. The goal-setting process is important for both short-term project-based or unit portfolios, but it is especially important for semester- or yearlong portfolios. Goal setting is a crucial step in portfolio development, because it forces students to monitor and reflect on their current learning and to self-adjust or remediate as needed for future learning. Goal setting occurs early in the portfolio process and can be revisited at appropriate intervals. This process helps the student take initiative to meet the checkpoint goals he sets for himself.

Academic goals play a major role in portfolios, but personal responsibility and interpersonal goals are equally important and necessary for students to succeed. Moreover, if students cannot meet their own goals, they need to develop a specific action plan that may require the help of peers, counselors, parents, or teachers, especially if they plan to meet their goals within a specific time frame. Students find it more manageable to break goals into two categories: short-term and long-term.

My Strengths and Problem Areas
Social Studies

Name: _Elrod_   Grade: _7_   Date: _Oct. 7_

My Strengths	Content/ Subject Matter	I loved studying about Egypt and I read three books on the pyramids. I feel like an expert.
	Processes (writing, reading, thinking, etc.)	I really like to read. Some of the books I select are high-school level but I have no problems with them. I also like writing creative stories.
	Social Skills (cooperation, behavior)	I am a good organizer in the groups and I always listen to others. Other group members respect my work.
My Problem Areas	Content/ Subject Matter	I receive low grades on research reports because I use only a few sources. I also tend to "copy" too much.
	Processes (writing, reading, thinking, etc.)	I can't spell anything. I proofread, but I can't look up every single word. I'm a creative writer but I can't stand using a dictionary or spellcheck.
	Social Skills (cooperation, behavior)	Sometimes I get impatient with my group. It takes too long for them to decide what to do! I'd rather do it myself sometimes because I can do a better job.

Figure 6.6

SkyLight Professional Development

Long-term goals such as reading ten books or participating in a library program require a significant amount of time to achieve. The time frame for long-term goals is usually at the end of a term or end of the school year.

Short-term goals, however, can usually be met by the date of the next portfolio conference. These goals constitute critical elements in a portfolio conference because the teacher and student discuss whether the student has met her goals from the last portfolio conference. The student is forced to reflect on why she did not meet her goals or find out what help she still needs and from whom in order to accomplish the goals. If she meets the goals, she can either extend the goals in a new direction or set totally new ones.

Strategies for the initial stages of student goal setting could start with a series of questions. Am I meeting the established criteria? Am I meeting my personal goals—both long-term and short-term? How do I self-inspect? How do I know I am on track? Both long- or short-term goal setting becomes an ongoing process. Students constantly assess and reassess where they have been, where they are, and where they are going. A goal-setting sheet helps students state what they plan to achieve in a specified time frame (See Figure 6.7 and the Examples page at the end of this chapter. For a form to use with students, see Blackline 6.6 at the end of this chapter.).

Review Criteria and Self-Assess—How Am I?

Students informally assess their work based on the criteria established, their reflections on individual pieces, and their inspection of the whole portfolio. By reviewing the standards and criteria, students make an informed decision about how they have fulfilled their goals by revisiting their checklists.

For a more formal assessment, a scoring rubric measures specific indicators under each score. Students review their own work and adjust as needed before they revise their portfolios or begin a new one. They analyze their own strengths and areas of concern and set short- and long-term goals to enhance their strengths and to improve their areas of concern.

THE PORTFOLIO CONNECTION

STUDENT GOAL-SETTING QUESTIONS:
- Am I meeting stated criteria?
- Am I meeting personal goals?
- How should I self-inspect?
- How will I know if I am on track?

Recent studies (Rolheiser 1996; Ross et al. 1999; as cited in Rolheiser et al. 2000) indicate that "student attitudes, effort, achievement, self-appraisal, and goal setting are enforced when students are taught self-evaluation techniques that enable them to attribute their success to personal actions, help them to identify concrete steps for improvement, and promote their own learning" (p. 35).

The inspection phase of portfolio development allows students to play a vital role in their learning and to "change the course" of their goals as they explore new directions, review their overall strengths and weaknesses, and evaluate future pathways for success. If students leave school still dependent on teachers to inspect their work, they have not developed into the independent thinkers and learners necessary to be successful in the twenty-first century.

Sample Goal-Setting Sheet

Name: _Chris_   Term: _2nd_

Subject: _Social Studies Term Project_   Date: _January 4_

Short-Term Goals	Target Date
1. Select project topic early.	January 10
2. Get to the library.	January 15
3. Create and use an outline.	January 30
4. Work with a partner to research online.	February 1

Long-Term Goals	Target Date
1. Include an interview with expert.	March 1
2. Read five historical fiction books on the topic.	March 30
3. Complete final project on time.	April 15

Date of Next Conference: _Feb 3_

Comment: _I won't procrastinate on this project like I did the last time._

Figure 6.7

Examples: Inspect to Self-Assess

Self-Assessment Checklist

☑ Self ☐ Peer ☐ Teacher

Student: _Ray_ Date: _April 11, 2001_

	Not Yet	Sometimes	Frequently
WORK HABITS:			
• Gets work done on time.	–	–	✓
• Asks for help when needed.	–	–	✓
• Takes initiative.	–	✓	–

Comments: *It's hard getting used to asking the group and teachers to help, but I'm getting better.*

	Not Yet	Sometimes	Frequently
STUDY SKILLS:			
• Organizes work.	–	–	✓
• Takes good notes.	–	✓	–
• Uses time well.	–	✓	–

Comments: *Since our base group has made this a goal, and we worked outside of class, I really am doing much better at this.*

	Not Yet	Sometimes	Frequently
SOCIAL SKILLS:			
• Works well with others.	–	–	✓
• Listens to others.	–	–	✓
• Helps others.	–	–	✓

Comments: *My group is great. We have really done good work on all our assignments. I've learned how to listen and help. My group has really helped me.*

Signed: _Ray_

Adapted from *How to Assess Authentic Learning* by K. Burke.
© 1999 SkyLight Training and Publishing. Used with permission.

Double-Entry Journal

Student Name: _Ray_ Grade: _7_
Subject: _Social Studies_

Starting My Portfolio	Finishing My Portfolio
Oh no! Another notebook to keep. I always manage to lose it before the end of the quarter. This time we have to show it to other people besides the teacher. I don't know how to type and I can't do artwork. I'm in big trouble!	I can't believe how hard I worked on this thing. I learned word processing because everyone else was typing theirs. I am pretty proud. Some of my friends read it and really liked it. My mom will love it. She'll probably show it to all the relatives.
I know I will have to become more organized or I'll fail!	I like the computer art work I added. It makes my portfolio look professional.
Date: _9/1_	Date: _11/3_

Analysis of My Strengths and Challenges

Old Me (Challenges)
- wrote one draft
- never proofread
- never showed work to others
- used verbal/linguistic intelligence
- never gave a thought to learning

New Me (Strengths)
- wrote 3 drafts
- use spell check
- have peers read everything
- use all eight intelligences
- reflect on my own thinking

I still need to improve in:

grammar
artwork
neatness
talking too much in groups
paraphrasing

Signed: _Ray_

Goal- Setting

Short-Term Goals (3 months)
1. Learn to use grammar check on computer.
2. Include 10 books in bibliography.
3. Learn to use the video camera.
4. Work on my interpersonal intelligence.

Ray's Goals

Long-Term Goals (6 months)
1. Learn to use computer graphics.
2. Take an art class as an elective.
3. Have someone in group tutor me in grammar.
4. Work on not interrupting others.

Target Date: _11/3_
(next portfolio conference)

Target Date: _5/8_
(final portfolio conference)

Comments: *I've decided I need to learn everything I can about technology (videos, computers) to succeed.*

Signed: _Ray_ Date: _11/5_

Chapter Six

Blackline Masters

Teacher Planner
Portfolio Inspection

Establish Criteria:

....
....

Create Checklists:

....
....

Self-Inspect
Learning Logs:

....

Learning Lists:

....

Reflective Journals:

....

Analysis of Strengths and Challenges:

....

Set Goals
Long-Term Goals:

....

Short-Term Goals:

....

Review Criteria and Self-Assess
Informal:

....

Formal:

....

Criteria Checklist

Name:_____   Grade:_____

Standard:_____

Benchmark/Descriptors:

	NOT YET 0	YES 1
• _____	____	____
• _____	____	____
• _____	____	____
• _____	____	____
• _____	____	____
• _____	____	____
• _____	____	____
• _____	____	____
• _____	____	____
• _____	____	____
• _____	____	____
• _____	____	____

Blackline 6.2

My Learning Lists

Name:_____ Class:_____ Date:_____

Vocabulary terms I have learned:

Things I have read:

Things I have written:

Things I am having trouble with:

Important things I have learned:

SkyLight Professional Development • www.skylightedu.com

Double-Entry Journal

Student:_____ Grade:_____

Subject:_____

Date: _____	Date: _____
Starting My Portfolio	**Upon Completion of My Portfolio**

Signed:_____ Signed:_____

Blackline 6.4

My Strengths and Challenges

Old Me
(Challenges)

New Me
(Strengths)

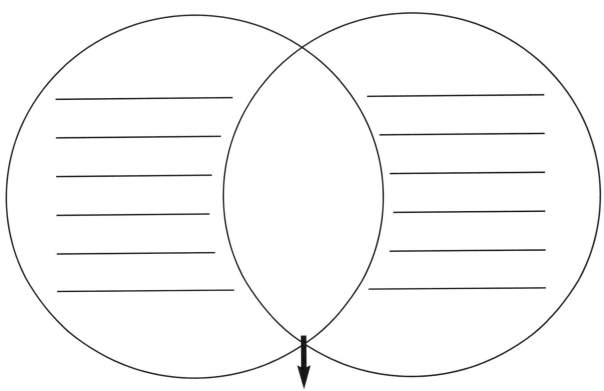

I still need to improve in:

Signed:_____ Date:_____

SkyLight Professional Development • www.skylightedu.com

Goal Setting

Short-Term Goals

Long-Term Goals

1. _____

2. _____

3. _____

4. _____

_____
name or picture

1. _____

2. _____

3. _____

4. _____

Target Date: _____
(next portfolio conference)

Target Date: _____
(final portfolio conference)

Comments:_____

_____

Signed: _____ Date: _____

Blackline 6.6

Reflect Metacognitively

Overview

Each piece included in the portfolio needs several metacognitive moments when students plan, monitor, and evaluate the value of the artifact, both as an individual piece and in relation to the whole portfolio (Belanoff and Dickson 1991). It is in this explicit reflection that students address the "learn to learn skills" embedded in the standards of learning. Rolheiser, Bower, and Stevahn (2000) define *reflection* as "ideas or conclusions that are a result of your thinking about your work. These ideas are connected to specific criteria and may help you determine future goals and actions" (p. 40). Among the learn to learn standards (see Figure 7.1) are skills necessary for

REFLECTIVE TOOLS:
- Planning
- Goal setting
- Self-assessment
- Self-monitoring
- Self-regulation
- Self-evaluation

Learn to Learn Standards

Students will demonstrate within and integrate across all content areas the ability to:

1. develop, monitor, and revise plans of action to meet deadlines and accomplish goals;

2. identify problems and define their scope and elements;

3. review and revise communications to improve accuracy;

4. apply acquired information, ideas, and skills to different contexts;

5. develop and apply strategies based on one's own experience in preventing and solving problems.

From *Show-Me Standards.* © 1993 by the Missouri Department of Elementary and Secondary Education.

Figure 7.1

problem solving and decision making in real-world situations. These reflective tools include: planning, goal setting, self-assessment, self-monitoring, self-regulation, and self-evaluation. These particular process standards fall into a category of cognitive skills often referred to as metacognition or the learn to learn skills.

One easy way to reflect on portfolio pieces is to tag or label each piece. The tag explains the value of the piece and why the piece has particular significance in the collection (Mills-Courts and Amiran 1991). These tag lines, labels, comments, and points provide a running monologue. This monologue brings the portfolio alive for the viewer who has not taken part in the development of the portfolio or who has not had an opportunity to discuss the portfolio with its creator. Samples of typical student reflections on items in the portfolio are displayed on the Examples page at the end of this chapter.

The portfolio offers robust opportunities for ongoing metacognitive reflection in three distinct ways. As students develop their portfolios, they survey the overall scheme for their portfolio and plan what their goals are. Then, they may shift automatically into a monitoring mode when each additional artifact is weighed against the whole portfolio. And, of course, students naturally evaluate as they reflect on just why the piece is valued and the reason it should be included in the finished portfolio (Burke 1992).

Digital Connection

The digitally-enhanced portfolio can effectively level the playing field for some children whose academic limitations in a traditional setting may be erased by computer applications. In these cases, digital portfolios assist others in recognizing these students' strengths and capabilities and "how they are smart," leading to a satisfying and pleasing outcome for all.

Introduction

The best research on cognitive development suggests that it is extremely important for students to think about their own thinking, and reflect on how they learn and why they fail to learn (Mills-Courts and Amiran 1991). When people use metacognition they can "describe the steps and sequences used before, during, and after problem solving" (Costa 1991, p. 23).

The creation of portfolios as viable assessment tools is in itself a marked improvement in evaluation methodology. The intrinsic value of the portfolio strategy, however, lies in the opportunity for metacognitive reflection by students as they plan, monitor, and

The portfolio fosters organizational skills as students devise a system for collecting artifacts in a regular and systematic way, and fosters higher-order tasks, such as predicting, prioritizing, and ranking.

evaluate themselves throughout the entire process, and as they uncover the reasons why they have included certain items in the portfolio. It is through this emphasis on self-monitoring and self-reflection that classroom assessment attains deeper dimensions. Student portfolios provide balance to the entire student assessment picture.

In terms of life skills, the portfolio is a wonderful decision-making tool for the student (Mills-Courts and Amiran 1991). It fosters organizational skills as students devise a system for collecting artifacts in a regular and systematic way, and it also fosters higher-order skills, such as predicting, prioritizing, and ranking. These are the real-word learnings that become an integral part of the portfolio process.

In this chapter, ideas for metacognitive reflection are explored in three stages.

1. In the planning stage students think ahead about the portfolio content and design.
2. In the monitoring stage students pay careful attention to details as the portfolio takes on a shape of its own.
3. In the evaluation stage students critically assess their work to ensure quality and accountability.

Within these three major categories a number of ideas are suggested. Some are quite obvious and easy to implement, while others are more abstract and require more thoughtful reflection.

THREE STAGES FOR METACOGNITIVE REFLECTION:

- **Planning**
- **Monitoring**
- **Evaluating**

Planning Stage

Visualization—Film Footage

One of the most powerful techniques for personal reflective planning is the ability to envision the desired goal or outcome (Fogarty and Bellanca 1989). Students can visualize a favorable reception of their artifacts by others. When students form this scenario in the mind's eye, they can shape their work to achieve that end. To help students become more skillful at visualizing complete and pleasing work included in their portfolios, teachers can have students practice recalling things and running through them in their minds. For example, students might try to visualize their final, showcase portfolio and the favorable comments of the viewer.

As students begin to work on their portfolios, the planning stages include setting goals about their learning and how that learning might be reflected in the portfolio. Many times, their written reflections grow out of their early visions of these goals. For example, one student reflection, taped to a drawing, stated, "Before I did this project, I envisioned what my invention would look like. This is the first sketch I made."

Strategic Planning—Road Map

A mental road map can be used to plot the route or process before embarking on a trip (Fogarty 1994). This helps students clarify their goals for each piece included in the portfolio. Naturally, this plan is embedded in the earliest steps of the portfolio development. However, like any dynamic process, as the portfolio begins to take shape it may not appear as the student originally envisioned. Therefore, the student may have to adjust and revise the strategic plan on occasion. This road map may take the form of a flowchart, a list, or a concept map, as the student writes or sketches a sequence of how the project will unfold. For a sample strategic plan, see the Examples page at the end of this chapter. For a form to use with students, see Blackline 7.1 at the end of this chapter.

> **CLUSTERING OR CHUNKING:**
> Separating criteria into sequential order so students progress in a logical order and complete one step at a time

Establishing Benchmarks—Chunking

A strategic plan implies the existence of clearly defined benchmarks along the way (Burke 1993). Portfolio development is a long-term project. With such an extensive undertaking, it is often best to lay out the plan in smaller, more manageable chunks. By "chunking" the project and establishing benchmarks, success is ensured. The chunking process is similar to what is used with research projects, lab reports, and robust performance tasks, as well as with portfolio development. Benchmarks may be established for collecting, selecting, and reflecting on the portfolio.

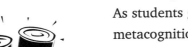

Monitoring Stage

Labeling—Soup Cans

As students gather and compile items, they employ their skills of metacognition. Specifically, as each item is scrutinized, an inner voice directs the activity, providing reflective comments about why a particular piece is valued. Labeling is a strategy that directs students to listen to that inner voice (Fogarty 1994). Labels can include a key phrase or comment that is placed either on or next to the artifact. See Figure 7.2 and the Examples page (at the end of this chapter) for samples of labels.

This initial labeling provides a quick inventory of what is included in the collection and gives insight about what is valued. To read a portfolio without reflections is like looking at a photo album without personalized comments. When someone takes the time to add that metacognitive monologue to the photo album, it is so much more engaging to the audience—and every portfolio has an audience!

Labeling

Figure 7.2

Bridging Questions

Asking key questions is a viable reflective technique for bridging ideas from one situation to another. For example, as students contemplate the various decisions about their portfolios, questions may help them clarify their purposes, selections, and presentation concerns. Students can ask themselves how and why questions to monitor their decisions:

- Why am I including this?
- How might I present this briefly, yet effectively?
- Why would this be essential?
- How can I eliminate some of these artifacts and still present a complete picture?
- Exactly what am I trying to convey?

This self-questioning helps students become more aware and explicit about the selection process and it helps keep them focused on the goals or standards they are trying to accomplish. A sample of bridging questions is provided on the Examples page at the end of this chapter. Blackline 7.2 provides bridging questions for students to use to reflect on items in their portfolio; Blackline 7.3 provides questions students can answer in the entry selection and creation process (both appear at the end of this chapter).

Evaluating Stage

Artifact Registry—Log-a-Line

Perhaps one of the easiest and most helpful metacognitive strategies is the portfolio registry (Dietz 1992). The registry provides an anecdotal record or biography of the work over time. As the student adds or deletes items from the portfolio during the project or the year, he or she may make a memo in the registry. This memo might include name, date, and a reason for including or excluding the artifact. (For a sample artifact registry, see the Examples page at the end of this chapter.) If the registries are kept up to date, the history of the portfolio is readily available for anyone to see.

> Asking key questions is a viable reflective technique for bridging ideas from one situation to another.

In fact, this registry often can provide insight into the decision-making process if the student plans to create a showcase portfolio from a working portfolio. The working portfolio usually has many more items than the final, showcase portfolio. This process involves a lot of decision making on the part of the learner.

Anecdotes—Story Time

Learning is embedded in stories and vignettes students tell. As students relay the stories behind the artifacts they have selected for their portfolios, learning comes alive for the learner and for the listener. Reflection is not always done solo, as some suspect. These dialogues provide a perfect forum for in-depth reflection by students as they think about their learning as evidenced in the portfolio entries. At regular intervals, as students add items to their portfolios, students may be asked to share the anecdote with one other student. Student pairs may take turns telling stories about the creation of their artifacts and anecdotal sharing can become a part of the portfolio development. See Figure 7.3 and Blackline 7.4 (at the end of the chapter) for appropriate story starters.

"My teacher said I'm riding along in a 'No Passing' zone!"

Story Starters

The metaphor . . .	One insight . . .
At least . . .	A reflection . . .
Compare to . . .	This symbolizes . . .
Looking back . . .	I assessed them . . .
The change I made . . .	One choice . . .
The problem I'm having . . .	A question I have is . . .
Three things I remember are . . .	To do this differently, I would . . .
My favorite part is . . .	If I had one more day, I would . . .

Figure 7.3

Metacognitive reflection is a crucial step in the portfolio process. Rather than completing each artifact when assigned and then forgetting about the skills and lessons learned while completing the assignment, reflection takes it one step further—students are made to remember each artifact's lesson and then place it in the context of the portfolio's purpose. Planning, monitoring, and evaluating each item in the portfolio and then reflecting on the portfolio as a whole allows students to absorb the entire scope of what they have learned. For a form to help plan the entire metacognitive process (planning, monitoring, and evaluating), see Blackline 7.5 at the end of this chapter.

Examples: Reflect Metacognitively

Planning
STRATEGIC PLAN

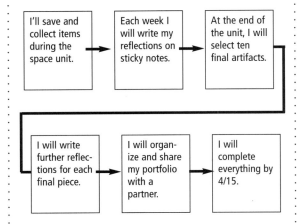

I'll save and collect items during the space unit. → Each week I will write my reflections on sticky notes. → At the end of the unit, I will select ten final artifacts.

I will write further reflec-tions for each final piece. → I will organ-ize and share my portfolio with a partner. → I will complete everything by 4/15.

Monitoring
LABELING

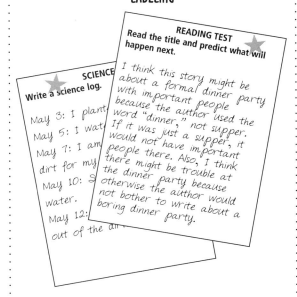

SCIENCE
Write a science log.

May 3: I plant...
May 5: I wat...
May 7: I am...
dirt for my...
May 10: S...
water.
May 12:...
out of the d...

READING TEST
Read the title and predict what will happen next.

I think this story might be about a formal dinner party with important people because the author used the word "dinner," not supper. If it was just a supper, it would not have important people there. Also, I think there might be trouble at the dinner party because otherwise the author would not bother to write about a boring dinner party.

Monitoring
BRIDGING

Now I ask myself . . .

1. Why am I including this?

   I feel that this is my strongest writing of the year.

2. Is this essential to my goal?

   Yes—my goal was to improve my writing skills this semester.

3. How might I connect this to what comes before? After?

   The entries before this one show how little effort I put into my writing. The entries after will show how my writing keeps improving!

Evaluating
ARTIFACT REGISTRY

IN	OUT	ARTIFACT	COMMENT
4/28	5/12	Puppet	It's a great project to tell about.
5/12		Videotape	Tape of puppet show is easier to store and show.
5/20	6/5	Letter to agency	Summarizes my goals.
6/2		*The Eagle* (School Newspaper)	My article on graffiti is in it.
6/5		Newsletter	Update the other one.

SkyLight Professional Development

Chapter Seven

Blackline Masters

Strategic Plan

Directions: In the boxes provided, write the specific steps or actions needed to reach your goal. Remember to include time frames or dates.

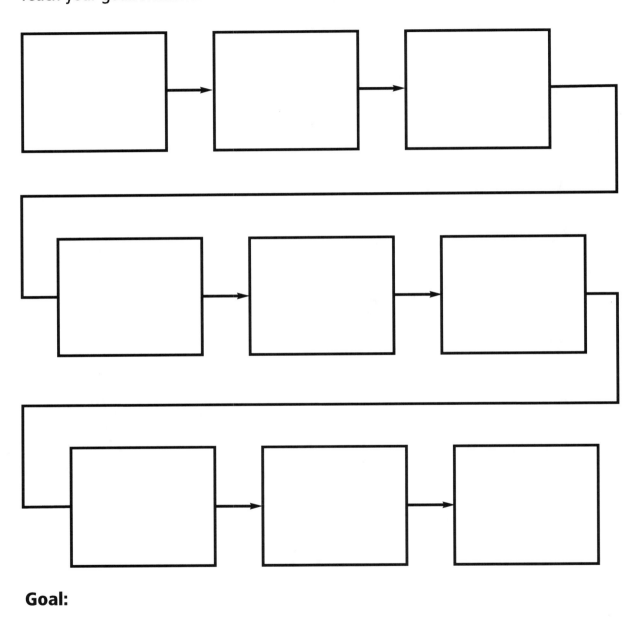

Goal:

_____

Blackline 7.1

SkyLight Professional Development • www.skylightedu.com

Sample Bridging Questions

Directions: Select some of these bridging questions or write your own to help you reflect on items in your portfolio.

1. Why have I chosen this piece?

2. What are its strengths? weaknesses?

3. Why is it important?

4. How and where does it fit in with what I already know?

5. What category does it fit into?

6. How might I label it appropriately?

7. What if I took it out of my portfolio?

8. How do I think others will react to it?

9. On a scale of 1–10, I give it a _____ because _____.

10. What question might someone ask me about this item?

11. How do I really feel about this?

12. Does this piece meet the standards?

Reflective Questions
Entry Selection and Creation

Select One Entry: _____

1. What standard did you meet?

2. What process did you use to complete the entry?

3. What problems did you encounter?

4. How did you solve those problems?

5. What did you learn by doing this entry?

6. What would you do differently if you did it again?

Signed: _____   Date: _____
(student)

SkyLight Professional Development • www.skylightedu.com

Story Starters for Individual Pieces in the Portfolio

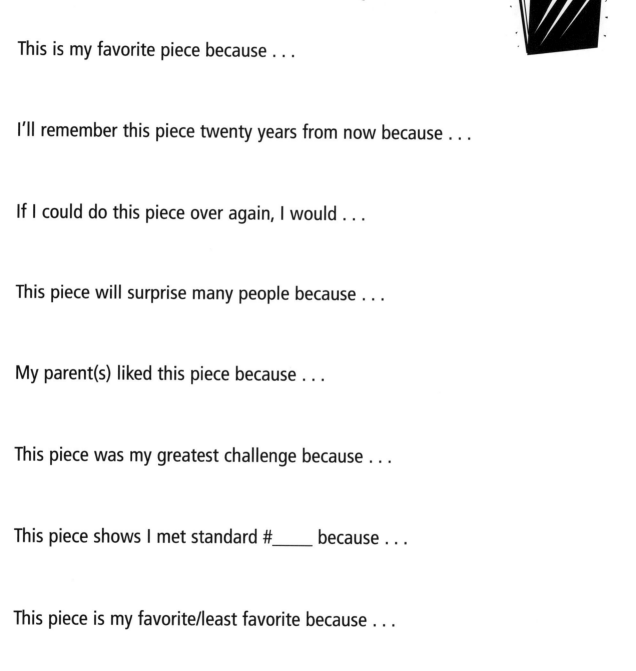

This is my favorite piece because . . .

I'll remember this piece twenty years from now because . . .

If I could do this piece over again, I would . . .

This piece will surprise many people because . . .

My parent(s) liked this piece because . . .

This piece was my greatest challenge because . . .

This piece shows I met standard #_____ because . . .

This piece is my favorite/least favorite because . . .

Blackline 7.4

Teacher Planner

Metacognitive Reflection

Think about each of these reflective tools and jot down one way you might use each of them with your students as they learn to plan, monitor, and evaluate their portfolio work.

Planning

Visualization

. . . .

. . . .

Strategic Planning

. . . .

. . . .

Establishing Benchmarks

. . . .

. . . .

Monitoring

Labeling

. . . .

. . . .

Bridging Questions

. . . .

. . . .

Evaluating

Artifact Registry

. . . .

. . . .

Anecdotes

. . . .

. . . .

Blackline 7.5

SkyLight Professional Development • www.skylightedu.com

Chapter 8

Perfect and Evaluate

Overview

In preparation for the portfolio conference with parents or other interested parties, both the student and teacher may want to perfect the portfolio by adding finishing touches to it. The content of the portfolio is critical, but the organization and visual appeal add to the overall effect and reflect the personality of the student. During this stage, students examine the entire portfolio for visual inconsistencies such as missing labels or tattered artifacts, or for refinements that might improve the outward appearance or the inherent meaning of particular artifacts. This is the time to spruce up the cover, check the registry for accuracy, and add artwork or design ideas. Adding this final flair makes the difference between a solid effort and an exemplary one. Teachers may use this stage to evaluate the portfolio, develop and apply scoring rubrics, and assign a grade or grades to the portfolio. A rubric is a set of scoring guidelines for evaluating student work. "The rubric answers an important question: What does mastery (and varying degrees of mastery) of a task look like? . . . The rubric must enable judges and performers to discriminate effectively between performances of different quality" (Rolheiser, Bower, and Stevahn 2000, p. 91). Although not every teacher will want to grade or be required to grade portfolios, it is helpful to understand the grading process and examine methods for summative evaluation. Even if the teacher does not grade the portfolio, the rubrics can be used for self-assessment and accountability for meeting standards.

> **RUBRIC:**
> a set of scoring guidelines for evaluating student work

Introduction

"Portfolios offer a way of assessing student learning that is quite different from traditional methods. While achievement tests offer outcomes in units that can be counted and accounted, portfolio assessment offers the opportunity to observe students in a broader context: taking risks, developing creative solutions, and learning to make judgments about their own performances" (Paulson et al. 1991, p. 63).

The issue to grade or not to grade portfolios is controversial. The key to understanding the options available is to review the purposes of the portfolio. If the purpose of the portfolio is to reflect on the students' best work, to establish a process and product for conferences, or to trace growth and development in an informal way, the portfolio does not need to be evaluated formally.

If the portfolio is tied to accountability, however, it is an important evaluation tool. Individual pieces or the portfolio as a whole need to be assessed according to predetermined performance standards and criteria for excellence. Kallick (1989) says learners have to "internalize external standards and expectations for good work and understand explicit ways to improve performance to meet those standards" (p. 313).

If the portfolio is used schoolwide, Wiggins (cited in Vavrus, 1990) suggests that colleagues decide on key items that represent important learning and set some standards for what constitutes excellent work and indicators that cover the range of students' needs, interests, or styles. Wortham (2001) suggests that the data collected by using informal or performance assessment should construct a holistic picture of a child and should show progress that can be reported to parents and school district administrators periodically throughout the year. She suggests that these alternative types of reporting "are more suitable for communicating the development and learning of children in the early childhood years" (p. 219).

Digital Connection

The evaluation of the digital portfolio will require the inclusion of scoring criteria related to the application of computer and telecommmunications tools students have used. A rubric with the criteria for designing the digital portfolios needs to be developed and provided prior to the initiation of the portfolio process.

Fun Rubric

Rubrics are useful tools for choosing criteria students must meet and for using the resulting rubric to assess student work. If students are not familiar with rubrics, teachers can introduce rubrics by taking students through the process of creating a fun rubric (see Figure 8.1). The teacher asks students to get into groups by lining up according to their birthdays. Once the students are in groups of five, the teacher asks them to select any fun topic to assess, such as a party, a movie, pizza, prom, recess, or school lunch.

Creating a Fun Rubric

1. Line up according to the month and day of your birthday.

2. Call out your birthday and section off in groups of five according to month and then day, if needed.

3. Roles:
   - Earliest Birthday: Organizer
   - Second Earliest: Materials Manager (newsprint and markers)
   - Third Earliest: Recorder (write)
   - Fourth Earliest: Reporter (share)
   - Last: Encourager—"Awesome" (help other members)

4. Task: Select a fun topic and create a rubric to assess it.

5. Time Limit: Twenty-five minutes

6. Sharing: Reporter shares rubric.

7. Processing: Value of doing a fun rubric first.

Figure 8.1   Adapted from Art Costa.

Teachers can show students the fun rubric for assessing a birthday party (Figure 8.2). The teacher may have to go over the birthday party rubric column by column to make sure the students understand the criteria and the indicators related to the criteria. Students should have twenty-five minutes to create their own fun rubric on big pieces of paper. When the students share their fun rubrics and talk about the process of writing rubrics, they will be internalizing the importance of criteria to determine degrees of quality.

No Grades

Many teachers, especially at the elementary level, feel grades cause students to focus more on "What did I get?" rather than "What did I learn?" They also feel that students' comfort level, willingness to take risks, and self-esteem increase when they are not worried about evaluations of their work. Some educators feel that eliminating grades from items in the portfolio encourages more honesty in peer comments and more constructive feedback from parents and teachers.

Rubric for Assessing a Birthday Party

	1 "I need to go home and do my homework!"	2 "Can't stay—I've got chores at home."	3 "Can I spend the night?"	4 "Will you adopt me?"
Food	steamed broccoli and carrots	Mom's tuna fish and potato chip casserole	McDonald's Happy Meal (free balloons)	super deluxe pizza (deep dish)
Gifts	new underwear (Kmart specials)	school supplies (Mr. Eraserhead)	*Tarzan* Video	Britney Spears CD
Entertainment	my sister's poetry readings (T.S. Eliot)	polka music (accordion rap song)	Blues Clues and Friends	N'Sync Live
Games	"Go Fish!" and "Slap Jack"	musical chairs to Broadway show tunes	virtual reality headsets	full contact Twister (no chaperones)

Figure 8.2

Adapted from *How to Assess Authentic Learning,* 3rd Edition, p. 87, by K. Burke.
© 1999 by SkyLight Training and Publishing, Inc. Used with permission.

Self-Assessment—I'm Growing!

Some portfolios are used to show students' growth and development over time, their reflections about their work, and their rationale for selecting specific pieces. Since this work reflects the students' choices, the portfolio is not graded. The teacher, parents, and peers, however, can provide oral and written comments to the students and the students can self-assess their own progress. For a sample evaluation, see the Examples page at the end of this chapter. For a form to use in the classroom, see Blackline 8.1 at the end of this chapter.

In this type of portfolio, individual effort and development are emphasized instead of comparisons with other students. Students with linguistic, learning, or behavioral challenges and students who prefer different learning styles usually feel good about their portfolio because it represents their personal favorites, demonstrates what they have learned in a variety of formats, and allows them to have fewer time constraints than with traditional tests and assignments. This type of portfolio provides a way to organize student learning into a manageable unit that provides a richer experience than hundreds of loose work sheets, drawings, or tests. It also provides a positive reinforcement for learning that may not be conveyed by traditional letter grades and standardized test scores.

SELF-ASSESSMENT PORTFOLIO:

- students choose work that shows growth over a certain period of time
- individual effort and development are emphasized
- teacher and parents provide comments on student progress

Graded

Some items included in the portfolio must be graded, such as tests and term papers. Assignments that are not subjective, such as mathematics problems, are usually given a grade. Some teachers and parents—and even students—feel that grades give students a goal to work toward. When deciding to grade items in a portfolio, there are several methods to choose from; it is important for teachers to decide what items will be graded and determine how they will be graded ahead of time.

Previously Graded Entries—What Did I Get?

Many portfolios contain a selection of items that may have been previously graded. The items have been turned in earlier in the quarter and assessed according to grading standards established by the district, teacher, and/or students. Sometimes the grading is done with rubrics—guidelines for giving scores based upon performance criteria and a rating scale. For example, if students receive a grade for creating a graph in mathematics, that grade would be in the grade book but the rubric could be attached to the graph (see Figure 8.3). Also see Blackline 8.2 at the end of this chapter.

Grade 8 Rubric for Algebra Data Analysis Using Inequalities

Illinois State Math Goal 8: Use algebraic and analytical methods to identify and describe patterns and relationships in data, solve problems, and predict results.

Task Description: The music store you work for has asked you to recommend what kind of music they should order for next month. They need information on what types of music are preferred by different age groups (under 10 yrs., teen, adults). You are to take a survey, display your results in a chart, include 3 types of graphs (triple bar, stem and leaf, and box and whisker plot) and write up a recommendation for your boss after you analyze this data.

Criteria	Indicators	0–1 Not Yet	2 Almost	3 Meets Expectations	4 Exceeds Expectations	Score
Format	• Has name, period on cover • Turned in on time	• No name • Not on time	• Has name, period • On time	NA	NA	
Web page	• Color title • Related graphics • Working links • Sources cited	Text only, 3–4 errors, incomplete footer and sources	Title, 2–3 errors, unrelated graphic, some sources cited	Title with color graphics, easy to read, 0–1 errors, all links work, sources cited	Superior attractive design that enhances topic, creative links, sources properly cited	
Overheads	• Colorful title slide includes graphs • Readable, no errors • Bibliography	Title page, no graphics, more than 3 errors, inaccurate graphs, and no bibliography	Title, some graphics, 2–3 errors, inaccurate graphs and bibliography	Title, graphics, graphs, 0–1 errors, bibliography	Creative title, appropriate graphics, accurate graphs, no errors, bibliography	
Graphs	• Break-even equation • Profit equation • Line graphs	Correct or partially correct display of only 1 of 3 types of equations/graphs	Partially correct display of 2 out of 3 types of equations/graphs	Visually appealing, correct display of all 3 types	Sophisticated display of all 3 types of graphs	
Written	• Evidence of reason • Supporting statistics	Unclear recommendation, no supporting data	Recommendation made without supporting data	Clear recommendation using supportive statistics	Insightful recommendation using supporting data	

Scale

A =	D =
B =	F =
C =	

Total Score _____

Comments:

Adapted from Jean Tucknott, Eisenhower Jr. High, Schaumburg District 54, IL and Margaret Novotny, St. Raymond School, Mount Prospect, IL. Used with permission.

Figure 8.3

Since all the work in this type of portfolio has already been graded, the portfolio is used to review student work, to trace growth and development, and to conduct conferences. Sometimes students revise and refine their previously graded work to improve the quality of their entries before sharing the portfolio with others. They can staple both copies together to show the corrections they have made along with the rubric to show whether or not they met standards. The reflective comments reveal students' intrapersonal feelings and the goals they set for future growth.

Key Items Selected for Grading—Roulette Wheel

Sometimes teachers tell the students in advance which entries will be graded after the portfolio is submitted. Teachers might select two items which they feel are important (e.g., research paper, cooperative project, oral presentation) and then allow students to select two or three other items to be graded. This method allows teachers to make sure key accountability pieces are included, while also allowing students to choose which pieces they feel represent their knowledge and understanding of the key concepts. It is important that the items be graded according to predetermined criteria and indicators developed by the teacher and students. Some teachers, however, choose another option. They do not tell the students which items they plan to grade until after the entire portfolio is submitted. These teachers want students to do quality work on all of the entries—not just the ones they know will be graded. Once the key items are selected, the teacher uses a rubric to grade the pieces fairly and consistently (see Figure 8.4 for a sample rubric for a student dramatization).

Each Entry Graded—One-to-One

Every item in the portfolio may be graded either prior to submitting the final portfolio or after the portfolio is submitted. The grades are determined by standards developed by the class and teacher or from scoring rubrics established by the school or district. The evaluation scale helps ensure consistency and fairness in the grading process. The advantage of this method is that students put a great deal of effort into all the entries since they know they will be evaluated.

Oral Presentation

Standard: The student gives an oral presentation.

Criteria	Not Yet 1	In Progress 2	Meets Standard 3	Exceeds Standard 4
Voice • Expression • Tone • Feeling	Used one element	Used two elements	Used three elements appropriately	Used all three elements effectively and enthusiastically
Volume	Could be heard by a few people in the room	Could be heard by people in front row only	Could be heard by most people in room	Could be heard clearly by all people in room
Enunciation	Could understand some words	Could understand most words	Could understand all of the words	Spoken like a professional actor
Content • Facts • Quotes • Statistics	• Used one element • Some inaccuracies	• Used two elements • Accurate information	• Used three elements • Accurate information • Current sources	• Used three elements • Accurate and current sources • Creative presentation

Figure 8.4

This type of portfolio often constitutes a large percentage of the total grade. Students usually know in advance what assignments will be graded and the criteria upon which they will be evaluated. The disadvantage for teachers is the time involved in assessing portfolios when they are submitted, especially in the middle school and high school where teachers teach as many as 150 students. Figure 8.5 is a sample evaluation of a videotaped speech from a portfolio. Another sample of a portfolio with individually graded items is provided on the Examples page at the end of this chapter.

Sample Speech Rubric

Name of Speaker **Eddie**

Title of Speech **My Summer in the Country**

VOLUME

I couldn't hear you.	It was hard to hear you.	I heard you most of the time.	You were easy to hear.
1	2	3	4

SCORE **3**

EYE CONTACT

You didn't use eye contact.	You hardly ever used eye contact.	Sometimes you made eye contact.	You had really good eye contact.
1	2	3	4

SCORE **2**

VISUAL

Foul Ball (You had no visual or it wasn't right.)	A Walk (Your visual was good, but you didn't use it.)	R.B.I. (Your visual made your speech better.)	Grand Slam (Your visual was very creative.)
1	2	3	4

SCORE **4**

FOCUS

 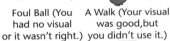

Muddy (I wasn't sure what you meant.)	Foggy (Sometimes I didn't know what you meant.)	Fuzzy (Most of the time I knew what you meant.)	Crystal Clear (I always knew what you meant.)
1	2	3	4

SCORE **3**

Comments: _Eye contact would have made your speech a hit! Creative use of visual aids—I loved the horse saddle! Great speaking voice, too._

Scale
14–16 = A
10–13 = B
7–9 = C
Below 6 = Not yet

Final Grade : **B**

Figure 8.5

174

Used by permission of Kris Walsh, a teacher from Palatine, IL.

SkyLight Professional Development

One Grade for Whole Portfolio—Blue Ribbon

Many teachers find that regardless of whether or not individual items in the portfolio are graded, they grade the whole portfolio on the basis of specific generic criteria such as creativity, completeness, organization, evidence of thoughtfulness, evidence of improvement, reflectiveness, and quality of work. (See the Examples page and Blacklines 8.3 and 8.4 at the end of this chapter for sample portfolio rubrics.) Teachers assign a letter grade, point value, or percentage grade based upon the organization of the entire portfolio. Grading the portfolio as a whole requires less time than grading each item individually, but it still provides specific feedback to the students. Sample criteria for grading portfolios follow.

SAMPLE CRITERIA FOR GRADING PORTFOLIOS

- Accuracy of information
- Completeness
- Connections to other subjects
- Creativity
- Development of process
- Diversity of selections
- Evidence of understanding
- Following directions

- Form (mechanics)
- Growth and development
- Insightfulness
- Knowledge of content
- Multiple intelligences
- Originality
- Persistence
- Quality product

- Reflectiveness
- Self-assessment
- Timeliness
- Transfer of ideas
- Variety of entries
- Visual appeal

Weighted Portfolio Rubric—And Justice for All

Items in a portfolio vary in their importance and, therefore, should be weighed appropriately when determining the student's final grade. Items can be weighed according to what the teacher and students feel are the most important elements, the major focus of learning, or the entries that showcase attainment of curriculum goals or standards. See Figure 8.6 and the Examples page (at the end of this chapter) for sample weighted rubrics for specific assignments. For a weighted rubric for the entire portfolio, see Blackline 8.5 at the end of this chapter.

SkyLight Professional Development

Weighted Rubric for Portfolio

Student: _Debbie W._   Subject: _Language Arts_ Date: _Jan. 24_

Goal/Standard: Use reading, writing, listening, and speaking skills to research and apply information for specific purposes in a portfolio.

Criteria	Indicators	1	2	3	4	Score
Form	• Spelling • Grammar • Sentence structure	2–3 errors	1–2 errors	0 errors	0 errors and a high level of writing	_4_ x 3 =_12_ (12)
Visual Appeal	• Cover • Artwork • Graphics	Missing 2 elements	Missing 1 element	All 3 elements included	All 3 elements are creatively and visually appealing	_3_ x 4 = _12_ (16)
Organization	• Completeness • Timeliness • Table of Contents	Missing 2 elements	Missing 1 element	All 3 elements included	All 3 elements demonstrate high level of organization	_4_ x 5 =_20_ (20)
Knowledge of Key Concepts	• Key concepts • Evidence of understanding • Application	No evidence of key concepts included in portfolio	Evidence of basic level of understanding of key concepts	Evidence of high level of understanding of key concepts	Evidence of ability to apply knowledge to new situations	_4_ x 6 =_24_ (24)
Reflections	• One per piece • Depth of reflection • Ability to self-assess	Missing 2 or more reflections	Missing 1 reflection	Insightful reflections for each piece	Reflections show insightfulness and ability to self-assess	_3_ x 7 =_21_ (28)

Comments:

Nice job! Next time, be sure to pay more attention to visual appeal and reflection.

Scale	
A=	_93–100_
B=	_87–92_
C=	_78–86_
D=	_below 78_

Final Score: _89/100_

Final Grade: _B_

Figure 8.6   From *How to Assess Authentic Learning*, 3rd Edition, p. 73, by K. Burke. © 1999 SkyLight Training and Publishing Inc. Used with permission.

Standards Portfolio—High Stakes

A few states are experimenting with portfolio assessment at the state level. These so-called high-stakes portfolios assess state standards achieved by the students. Outside scorers assess the portfolios using scoring rubrics that have been developed by psychometricians and teachers to increase the reliability of the scoring process. The portfolio includes required entries that demonstrate that the student has met certain requirements.

Combination Portfolio—Potpourri

Teachers can also experiment with grading options or alternate them at different times of the year and for different purposes and types of portfolios. Standardized rubrics from school systems, districts, and states serve as models and preparation guidelines to enable teachers to align classroom expectations and assessments with standardized expectations and assessments. Using global rubrics helps teachers set expectations correlated to other students in the district or state—not just in their own school.

> **EVALUATIING PORTFOLIO OPTIONS:**
> - No grades
>   - Self-assessment
> - Graded (using rubrics)
>   - Previously graded
>   - Key items graded
>   - Each entry graded
>   - One grade for portfolio

Guidelines for Grading Portfolios

Regardless of whether or not portfolios are graded or whether teachers or outside evaluators evaluate the contents, portfolios present a portrait of a student as a learner that cannot be captured by checklists, anecdotal records, or report cards. According to Vavrus (1990), "The key to scoring a portfolio is in setting standards relative to your goals for student learning ahead of time. Portfolios can be evaluated in terms of standards of excellence or on growth demonstrated within an individual portfolio, rather than on comparisons made among different students' work" (p. 48). In other words, portfolio evaluation is more similar to criterion-referenced tests than to norm-referenced tests.

THE PORTFOLIO CONNECTION

One of the major purposes of portfolios is to trace a student's progress. The student may never pass the state test, meet the state standards, or earn an "A." The portfolio shows the student's entry level and the progress he or she made. If a student started at a zero or "not yet" and progressed to a level two, he or she demonstrated growth toward meeting the goal or standard. The student, parent, and teacher should celebrate the journey thus far and establish new goals to motivate the student to improve. The guidelines in Figure 8.7 provide a framework for scoring portfolios. Teachers can adjust the guidelines to meet their purposes for scoring the portfolio. It is important, however, to share the scoring guidelines with the students *before* they complete their portfolio. They need to know the expectations for quality work.

Guidelines for Scoring Portfolios

1. Make sure the portfolio is correlated with curriculum goals or standards.

2. Introduce the portfolio by telling students why they will be doing it and what the intended goal is (final grade, reflection, standards, integration).

3. Show examples of portfolios. (Try to show examples that are "not yet," some that are "o.k." as well as some that are "awesome.")

4. Brainstorm a list of criteria that make up a portfolio (organization, reflection, connections, insights, goal setting).

5. Generate a list of indicators that specify the types of performances under each of the examples.

6. Create a scale that lists the indicators of each of the criteria on the scale (not yet, o.k., awesome; below expectations, meets expectations, exceeds expectations; or 1, 2, 3, 4).

7. Give students some choice in their selection of items to include.

8. Have students prepare portfolios.

9. Share the portfolios with the class or outside audience (other classes, teachers, parents, exhibitions).

10. Ask peers to give feedback on portfolios.

11. Have the students self-evaluate by using a rubric to score their own portfolios.

12. Use the portfolio rubric to complete a teacher evaluation.

13. Discuss the portfolios with the students.

14. Provide feedback.

15. Determine a grade based on self-evaluations and teacher evaluations.

16. Have the student set new goals for his or her next portfolio.

Figure 8.7

Examples: Perfect and Evaluate

Final Portfolio
(NO GRADES)

Student: _Jim B._   Grade: _3rd_   Date: _June 1_

Selection	Teacher Comments
1. Problem-solving log	You used several methods to solve the problems.
2. Book report video interview	Your answers to the questions I asked were thoughtful and creative.
3. Artwork	Try to use more color and graphics in your work.
4. Peer-edited short story	The comments others made really helped your story.
5. Cassette of the reading	Your fluency and speed have improved.
6. Science experiment drawing	The explanation of your drawing hit the standard.

Final Portfolio
(EACH ITEM GRADED)

Student: _Carol D._   Class: _Geometry_   Date: _May 26_

Selections	Grade	Comments
1. Geometric drawings	95	You have done a beautiful job drawing and labeling the angles.
2. Research report on "Why Math"	89	The research you did on the relevancy of math helped you see its importance.
3. Reflective journals	90	Your frustration on tests is evident from your journal. You seem to be working through your anxiety.
4. Profile of math-related professions	90	You made the transfer of math from the classroom to the outside world.
5. Student self-evaluation for course	91	I gave myself a 91 because I like math, but I still can't solve problems on my own.
Total Points 455 ÷ 5 = 91	91	It's interesting that your average is the same as your own self-evaluation!

Comments: Your writing and research skills and appreciation of why math is important are excellent. Even though you feel math is your weakest subject, you are making great strides to overcome your phobia and solve problems.

Suggested Future Goals: Work with your group more. Ask them to "talk out loud" when they are solving problems so you can see their thought processes.

Average grade for class work = 83 (33%)
Average grade for quizzes and tests = 85 (33%)
Final portfolio grade = 91 (34%)
Final grade for class = 86—B

Adapted from *How to Assess Authentic Learning*, 3rd ed. by K. Burke.
© 1999 SkyLight Training and Publishing, Inc. Used with permission.

One Grade for Entire Portfolio Rubric

	None 1	In Progress 2	Meets Expectations 3	Exceeds Expectations 4	Total Score
Organization					
1. Creative cover		✓			2
2. Self-assessment				✓	4
3. Completion of all items				✓	4
Visual Appeal					
1. Layout			✓		3
2. Art/graphics				✓	4
3. Creativity			✓		3
Evidence of Understanding					
1. Knowledge of subject			✓		3
2. Reflections				✓	4
3. Application of ideas				✓	4
Form					
1. Sentence structure			✓		3
2. Grammar			✓		3
3. Spelling/punctuation				✓	4

Scale: 45–48 = A
39–44 = B
34–38 = C
0–33 = Not Yet

Total: **41**

Final Grade: B

Weighted Rubric

Name: _Mary_   Date: _May 23_
Piece of Writing: _Persuasive Paper_

Score (1–5)   Score: 1___2___3___4___5___
Low   High

CONTENT	Score 4 x 7 = 28
• evidence or reason	(5 x 7 = 35)
• key ideas covered	
⊙ appropriate quotes –Not enough	
• supportive statistics	
• topic addressed	

ORGANIZATION	Score 5 x 6 = 30
• creative introduction	(5 x 6 = 30)
• thesis statement	
• appropriate support statements	
• effective transitions	

USAGE	Score 3 x 5 = 15
⊙ correct subject-verb agreement –2 errors	(5 x 5 = 25)
• no run-ons, fragments, or comma splices	
• correct verb tense	
• mix of simple and complex sentences	

MECHANICS	Score 5 x 2 = 10
• few or no misspellings	(5 x 2 = 10)
• correct use of punctuation	
• correct use of capitalization	

	TOTAL SCORE: 83
Scale: 93–100=A, 87–92=B, 78–86=C	100

Comments: _Your content and organization are good, but you need to work on your sentence structure. You had two plural subjects that had singular verbs._

Chapter Eight

Blackline Masters

Final Portfolio

(No Grades)

Student:_____ Grade:_____ Date:_____

Selection	Teacher Comments
1.	
2.	
3.	
4.	
5.	

Scoring Rubric

Select an item in the portfolio and create a rubric to grade it.

Standard: _____

Assignment: _____

CRITERIA	INDICATORS	1	2	3	4	SCORE
1.						___ x5 $\overline{(20)}$
2.						___ x5 $\overline{(20)}$
3.						___ x5 $\overline{(20)}$
4.						___ x5 $\overline{(20)}$
5.						___ x5 $\overline{(20)}$

SCALE

A=
B=
C=
D=

Final Score: _____ $\overline{(100)}$

Final Grade: _____

Comments:

Blackline 8.2

Portfolio Rubric

Student:_____ Subject:_____ Date:_____

❏ Self-Evaluation ❏ Peer Evaluation ❏ Teacher Evaluation

Criteria	1 Meets Some Requirements	2 Meets Most Requirements	3 Meets All Requirements	Score
A. Organization				
1. Completeness	Some entries are missing or incomplete.	All entries are completed according to directions.	All entries are completed and organized correctly.	
2. Visual Appeal (cover, graphics, artwork, layout)	Key elements are missing or elements meet minimum standards.	Key elements demonstrate originality.	Key elements demonstrate creativity and style.	
3. Format (spelling, punctuation, grammar, usage, typing)	Entries contain several written or proofreading errors.	Entries are error free.	Entries demonstrate high level of usage and writing skills.	
Comments:				
B. Evidence of Understanding				
1. Knowledge of Key Concepts	Entries reflect recall and comprehension.	Entries reflect analysis and synthesis.	Entries reflect evaluation and application.	
2. Process	Entries reflect basic understanding.	Entries reflect advanced understanding.	Entries reflect advanced understanding and transfer.	
Comments:				
C. Growth and Development				
1. Social Skills	Entries demonstrate minimum use of listening, sharing, and team work.	Entries demonstrate active involvement in group activities.	Entries demonstrate transfer of social skills to all class work.	
2. Problem Solving	Entries demonstrate ability to identify problems.	Entries demonstrate ability to brainstorm possible solutions.	Entries demonstrate ability to solve problems creatively.	
Comments:				
D. Metacognition				
1. Reflections	Reflective pieces meet minimum requirements.	Reflections provide insight into student's feelings.	Reflections provide evidence of insight and thoughtfulness.	
2. Self-Assessment	Self-assessment meets minimum requirements.	Self-assessment is based on reflections.	Self-assessment is based on reflection and rubric.	
3. Goal Setting	Statement of goals meets minimum requirements.	Goals are based on reflections.	Goals are based on reflections and self-assessment.	
Comments:				

Blackline 8.3

Adapted from *Designing Professional Portfolios for Change*, p. 129–130, by K. Burke.
© 1997 by SkyLight Training and Publishing Inc. Used with permission.

SkyLight Professional Development • www.skylightedu.com

Portfolio Rubric

Name:_____ Subject:_____ Grade:_____

Directions: Develop criteria and indicators for assessing the final portfolio.

Criteria	Does Not Meet Expectations 1	In Progress 2	Meets Expectations 3	Exceeds Expectations 4
1.				
2.				
3.				
1.				
2.				
3.				
1.				
2.				
3.				
1.				
2.				
3.				

Comments:

Scale
A = _____
B = _____
C = _____
D = _____

Final Score:_____

Final Grade:_____

Blackline 8.4

Weighted Rubric for Portfolio

Student:_____ Subject:_____ Date:_____

Goal/Standard:_____

_____

Criteria	Indicators	1	2	3	4	Score
Form	• Spelling • Grammar • Sentence structure	2–3 errors	1–2 errors	0 errors	0 errors and a high level of writing	__ x 3 =___ (12)
Visual Appeal	• Cover • Artwork • Graphics	Missing 2 elements	Missing 1 element	All 3 elements included	All 3 elements are creatively and visually appealing	__ x 4 =___ (16)
Organi-zation	• Complete-ness • Timeliness • Table of Contents	Missing 2 elements	Missing 1 element	All 3 elements included	All 3 elements demonstrate high level of organization	__ x 5 =___ (20)
Knowledge of Key Concepts	• Key concepts • Evidence of under-standing • Application	Little evidence of key concepts included in portfolio	Evidence of basic level of understand-ing of key concepts	Evidence of high level of understand-ing of key concepts	Evidence of ability to apply knowl-edge to new situations	__ x 6 =___ (24)
Reflections	• One per piece • Depth of reflection • Ability to self-assess	Missing 2 or more reflections	Missing 1 reflection	Insightful reflections for each piece	Reflections show insight-fulness and ability to self-assess	__ x 7 =___ (28)

Comments:

Scale

A=_____
B=_____
C=_____
D=_____

Final Score:_____
100

Final Grade:_____

From *How to Assess Authentic Learning*, 3rd Edition, p. 73, by K. Burke.
© 1999 SkyLight Training and Publishing Inc. Used with permission.

SkyLight Professional Development • www.skylightedu.com

Respect and Celebrate Accomplishments

Overview

A portfolio, by definition, is a container in which to hold things. It is implied that the container is used to carry the items for others to see and value. It is increasingly agreed that the primary purpose of portfolios in schools today is to enhance the assessment of the learning process. By including the actual artifacts that show evidence of students' development and achievement of learning standards, portfolios extend the assessment process beyond test scores or grade point averages. The value and many uses for student portfolios become apparent at all grade levels as they are used in more and more schools.

With the accomplishment of portfolios—print and electronic—students, teachers, and parents recognize the communication impact that they provide. Students want to show their portfolios to the outside world. As the potential of this value beyond the classroom is recognized, teachers look for effective ways to connect their students' accomplishments to interested audiences, such as parents, administrators, families, other students, and teachers.

The portfolio showcase or exhibition has evolved into an artistic, technological, and educational event. Students can skillfully present their work and communicate their learning dispositions and talents to others. The portfolio showcase and exhibition brings each student's work and accomplishments alive. As students present their pieces to others, they celebrate and enjoy their accomplishments while the viewers gain valuable insight into the students' "heads" about their understanding of what they have learned.

Portfolio showcases and exhibitions are viable tools to gain new understanding of students' accomplishments or new connections to learning and development. The student exhibitors trade places with their peers during the portfolio showcase. They have the opportunity to become reflective participants in the process of valuing and respecting their peers' work and growth. Those interested not only view the work, but also scrutinize the work and offer informed critiques of their assessments. Students also have the opportunity to receive input from others as they present their works in a three-way portfolio conference with the teacher and their parents. The intricacies of the portfolio surface as the dialogue unfolds.

It is increasingly agreed that the primary purpose of portfolios in schools today is to enhance the assessment of the learning process.

Introduction

"Evaluation continues the spirit of inquiry by providing one more chance to ask questions—and one more opportunity to learn. Evaluation occurs as learners take reflective stances in relation to their work and then invite others in to have conversations about it" (Crafton, cited in Crafton and Burke 1994, p. 5).

As teachers begin the portfolio development process, the role of student reflection and inquiry becomes apparent. Through portfolio conferences, exhibitions, and showcases, students' activities in acquiring knowledge and capacities for self-reflection on learning processes culminate in the true essence of portfolios: to value. Through ongoing critiques and conversations about the portfolio, students develop the capacity to become truly reflective learners "who always act with intention" (Harste et al. 1984). This stage helps students move beyond test-taking skills to gaining reflective inquiry skills. The portfolio exhibition "allows students to demonstrate their ability to apply knowledge and skills in authentic contexts" (Ferrara and McTighe 1992, p. 341).

If teachers encourage their students to become more thoughtful in reviewing learning standards, setting goals, and writing reflections, the conferences will generate lively discussions. As reflective inquiry occurs through conversations with teachers, peers, and others, students learn to see their learning experiences in different ways. The very art of explaining their learning helps students rehearse and reinforce their understanding.

Portfolio conferences range from simple, one-on-one dialogues between students and teachers, or students and parents, to formal exhibitions that promote student conversations about the contents of the portfolio with varied audiences. In portfolio showcases, students have the opportunity to select their finest, most improved or most significant accomplishments in a way that celebrates and acknowledges their academic growth. Whether conferences are basic, complex, face-to-face, or Web-based, they need to be well planned, monitored, and evaluated to be effective.

THE PORTFOLIO CONNECTION

When planning for portfolio conferences and exhibitions, teachers recognize that this is the time when "the rubber meets the road" and the critics come to the showing. The portfolio presentation is when the creator makes his or her work come alive. To effectively plan portfolio conferences, teachers first need to consider the purposes that best meet their students' needs and learning dispositions. Next, they make decisions about who the audience will be and when the conferences will take place. Once this is determined, they are ready to engage students in the conference planning process. Some considerations necessary to prepare for the presentation of portfolios are the allotted time frame, media (technology) options, personal style, and other concerns. At this point the *how* of the conference can be mapped out:

What will the goals be?
- Is the presentation for a peer conference or a student-led parent conference?
- Is the presentation for a class exhibition or a schoolwide portfolio showcase?
- Is the presentation for a college or a job interview?

What reflections do learners need to engage in?
- Will students need to compare their achievement to benchmarks and learning standards?
- Will the portfolio need to show progress over time?
- Will it show achievement of individual learning goals?

What questions should they prepare for their audience?
- Who is the audience?
- What are they looking for?
- How are they going to view the work?
- Are they familiar with the type of work?
- What can be done to maximize interest and understanding?

How do they wish to evaluate the conferences?
- Is there a particular format and scoring rubric to follow?
- Will they evaluate the contents and the reflections?
- Will they focus on social skills and communication?
- Will they evaluate the audience's reaction to what they learned about the students as readers, writers, thinkers, problem solvers, etc.?

SkyLight Professional Development

Also part of mapping out the how of the conference is to plan the logistics. Dates need to be scheduled and setup needs to be arranged. The time frame should also be determined. Will there be time for the "full metal jacket" or just a "Ready? Aim. FIRE!" approach? What technology media will be used? Is there a video segment or an audiotape that needs to be included? If media is part of the presentation, how is it to be incorporated in the overall plan?

Strategies for introducing the portfolio or inviting questions from the audience need to be carefully considered with the students so they can be prepared ahead of time. Here, the personal style of each student presenter needs to be considered. While engaged in peer portfolio conferences, students should be encouraged to use the opportunity to practice the art of anticipating the types of questions that will be asked about their portfolio entries and formulating appropriate responses. This is especially important when students are preparing digital portfolios for publishing on a Web site.

> **CONFERENCE PLANNING:**
> - Consider purpose of portfolio and conference/exhibition
> - Decide who the audience will be
> - Choose when
> - Map out what and how
> - Schedule dates and time
> - Plan setup

Students respond positively to brainstorming the possibilities for sharing educational portfolios with others. For example, students select an appropriate type of presentation, rehearse as needed in front of a mirror, and practice with a trusted friend or relative. The same ongoing teacher guidance that earlier supported the self-reflection process prepares students for portfolio conferences, exhibitions, and showcases. Students determine how to present each artifact or the overall content of their portfolios to their audiences in the most engaging and informative methods. Through the conversations at portfolio conferences and exhibitions, the student demonstrates that he or she has become a reflective and independent learner "who self-initiates, problem solves, reflectively evaluates her learning, collaborates, and shows concern for, and engages in complex thinking strategies" (Crafton 1991, p. 94).

For help in planning the portfolio conference, you may use Blacklines 9.1 and 9.2 at the end of this chapter.

Why Have Portfolio Conferences?

Portfolio conferences allow people other than the student and the teacher to see and discuss a student's work. Portfolios also provide real evidence of the accomplishment of schoolwide or districtwide objectives. In addition, portfolio conferences promote student goal setting and achievement-focused communication among teachers and parents. Most importantly, they engage students in meaningful reflection, inquiry, and discussion about their own learning processes. The following ideas can help guide teachers in considering the purpose, audiences, number, nature, and outcomes of portfolio conferences.

Portfolio conferences engage students in meaningful reflection, inquiry, and discussion about their own learning processes.

Promote Ongoing Student Evaluation and Goal Setting—On and On

Teachers plan for ongoing peer conferences with students or between students when they wish to promote student evaluation and inquiry into student learning processes. These ongoing peer conferences can promote student monitoring of their progress toward individual goals. "Despite all the testing that we do, both formal and informal, only the learner really knows what has been learned" (Howell and Woodley, cited in Goodman et al. 1992, p. 87).

Promote Student-Teacher Communication

Teachers who value students' dialogue about learning and achievement schedule regular individual conferences where students select artifacts, describe their significance, and reflect on their feelings. These conferences help students review their accomplishments, "recognizing how successful they were, and facilitating new experiences where they can apply their learning" (Silvers 1994, p. 27).

Promote Student-Student Communication

When portfolios include evidence from contributing members of learning teams, the portfolio conference's dialogue focuses on the quality of the learning community. Groups of students work together to present exhibitions or showcases of their significant achievement of learning goals as team members. Here, students become critical inquirers of their classroom's shared goals and purposes. They reflect on the progress they make developing a community, engaging in positive social interaction, solving problems, and resolving conflicts. They evaluate their progress as active learners and contributors to the shared achievement of academic goals and standards in projects and performances. These group-based conferences engage individual students in reflecting upon the impact of the social and cognitive skills that are promoted in the cooperative learning community and that are also important for life outside of the classroom.

Promote Student-Parent-Teacher Communication—Threesomes

The portfolio allows the student to become a significant part of the parent-teacher conference. When the student enters the dialogue, the parent-teacher conference becomes more learner-centered. In effect, it has become a student-led parent conference. When the student plans, conducts, and evaluates the presentation of portfolio entries to parents, the teacher takes a secondary role. In reality, the teacher facilitates the dialogue between parent and student at key places, but encourages the student to assume responsibility for the conference's success. The students are ultimately responsible for their own learning and should not have to rely on the teacher alone to talk "about" their learning.

PORTFOLIO CONFERENCES PROMOTE:
- Ongoing student evaluation and goal-setting
- Communication
- Teacher accountability
- Parental satisfaction
- Links to community

Promote Teacher Accountability—High Standards

In schools where teachers are required to provide clear and compelling evidence of student achievement, portfolio conferences can be scheduled for students and teachers, as well as school faculty and administrators. These conferences focus on portfolio entries that demonstrate the accomplishment of learning standards, the quality of academic products and performances, the depth of reflections, and the significance of the learning. These portfolio conferences connect the parallel processes of standards-based instruction with students' authentic learning.

Promote Parental Satisfaction

As schools move toward learner-centered curricula and inquiry-based learning, one of the greatest challenges is informing parents of these practices and explaining the professional and scientific knowledge base that supports these practices. Portfolio conferences address the concerns of parents by demonstrating their child's overall learning and achievement in the context of the instructional methodologies.

Portfolio conferences enable parents to learn about standards and curricular goals as they view and hear about their child's real learning experiences. They see evidence of authentic learning that includes products from hands-on activities, increasingly difficult problem-solving activities, and successful teamwork. While interviewing their children as they display artifacts of learning during the portfolio conferences and exhibitions, parents are given the opportunity to see the connection between the active learning process and learning. Parents become less cautious, more trusting, and often more enthusiastic about the transformation from traditional to engaged school curriculum. Students who are given the opportunity to lead the examination of their portfolios become convincing ambassadors of a school's success in meeting rigorous learning standards at all levels.

Accompany Communitywide Exhibitions

The portfolio conference in the form of an exhibition or showcase is instrumental in promoting important connections among students and parents, family and community members, and concerned local business people. Community-wide exhibitions and showcases offer the potential to reestablish the critical links between schools and families and between schools and communities.

As teachers and students become more confident with portfolio assessments and conferences, schoolwide exhibitions may become as commonplace as the science fair. Technology makes it possible to create computer-stored, Web-based portfolios of students' written work and multimedia presentations. Some school districts already provide selected showcases of students' portfolios on their district or school Web site. The impact of this medium in communicating the success of schools to the wider community will continue to grow.

SkyLight Professional Development

Technology helps teachers combine computer software with visual and auditory media that transforms student work into digital portfolio files. Laser-disc video will make it possible for students to conduct portfolio conferences with community members or pen pals from across the world. Teachers can use handheld scanners to collect and download information on student learning as they are engaged in it. Teachers can store checklists, anecdotal observations, and self-evaluations in minutes. Such breakthroughs lend an air of expectancy to the possibility of better engaging students, teachers, parents, and community members in a dialogue throughout the learning process—especially at portfolio conferences.

What Is the Focus of the Conference?

Significant Achievement—It Counts!

These conferences give students the opportunity to present portfolios of their significant achievements across selected areas of the curriculum. These might include pieces that promote student reflection on teacher-graded work, selected learning logs, projects or performances, or significant improvements in standardized test scores.

Goal Setting—Goal Post

The focus for these conferences is on students' previously set goals and include reflections and self-assessments of how they have reached their goals. Portfolios include pieces that highlight how the student has matched, met, or surpassed his or her goals. In some instances, the student needs to select a "not yet" piece and discuss the strategies she will employ to achieve the goal in the future.

Single Learning Process Areas—Invitational

Students compile portfolio artifacts that reflect each indicator of a certain process, such as becoming an effective writer, for these conferences. Students use the standards and criteria originally applied to scoring and reflect on how they have developed in these areas. They can include several artifacts to represent different audiences and invite responses through conference guides created ahead of time.

Personally Satisfying Pieces—I Like It!

Students select pieces that are most satisfying to them as learners and use this conference to display how they have grown as readers, writers, group members, intelligent thinkers, or overall students. While the portfolio pieces they share in the conferences may represent many or a few of the subject areas or learning processes, the pieces represent achievements about which the students feel best.

Joint Work—Join In

These portfolio conferences often are used in exhibitions and showcases to communicate the group, class, or schoolwide purposes. Students present how they have succeeded as communities of learners in a variety of cooperative/collaborative projects and experiences.

Overall Portfolio—The Big Picture

This is, perhaps, the most important conference because it requires the student to reflect on and self-assess strengths, weaknesses, successes, and failures across the curriculum. This conference represents the holistic picture of his performance and disposition toward learning. In this conference, the student calls attention to those pieces that best represent him throughout all the selected areas. The student may write a reflective summary for each selection, or create a conference guide that explains his characteristics as a learner. The big picture encourages students to value and celebrate the many ways in which they are developing as learners.

Digital Connection

The digital portfolio excels in its application to maintaining student portfolios over time. The ease of use that technology provides in selecting, updating, copying, and editing artifacts is a large improvement over the paper portfolio. The storage of the digital portfolio as files in zip diskettes or CDs is also seen as an enhancement of the portfolio process.

Who Is Involved and When Do They Conference?

After choosing the purpose and focus of the portfolio conference, the teacher and students decide who will participate in the conference and when. Portfolio conferences blend seamlessly with traditional parent conferences or end-of-the-grading periods in curriculum and instruction. Depending on the purpose, teachers may select the who and when of portfolio conferences from a full palette of choices (see Figure 9.1).

Possibilities for the Who and When of Portfolio Conferences

Connections to Authentic Learner Involvement—Connecting

Student-Student	Monthly
Pen Pal/Tech Pal	Quarterly
Multiage Students	By Semester
Student-Parent-Teacher	Quarterly
Portfolio Exhibition/Showcase—Everyone	Year-End

Teacher Accountability—Accounting for Learning Standards

Student-Teacher	Monthly
Student-Parent-Teacher	Quarterly
Student-Parent	By Semester
Portfolio Exhibition/Showcase—Everyone	Year-End

Parental Satisfaction with Learner Performance—Pleasing

Student-Teacher	Monthly
Student-Student	Quarterly
Student-Parent Home Conferences	By Semester
Student-Parent-Teacher	Quarterly
Portfolio Exhibition/Showcase—Everyone	Year-End

Outside Evaluations of the Success of Teaching and Learning—Evaluating

Student-Student (Cooperative Group Members)	Monthly
Multiage Student	Bimonthly
Student-Parent Home Conferences	By Semester
Significant Other	Quarterly
Pen Pal/Tech Pal	Quarterly
Schoolwide/Communitywide Portfolio Exhibitions/Showcase—Everyone	Year-End

Figure 9.1

How Does the Conference Happen?

To effectively prepare for the portfolio conference, students and teachers must construct a plan. Together they do everything from choosing conference goals to designing invitations to rehearsing conference dialogue to planning evaluations.

Choose Conference Goals—Scoring the Goal

Getting the portfolio ready is only one part of the story. To plan the most effective presentation, the goal must be clearly defined. Is the primary goal one of self-evaluation and self-reflection through the sharing with peers or parents? Is the primary goal a summative evaluation by the teacher? Is the goal to inform and impress a third party about the talent of the person presenting the portfolio? Whatever the goal may be, students need to zero in on it. The student may use this formula to set his or her goal:

1. Write the goal in a journal or notebook to clarify it in your mind.
2. Dialogue with a partner to articulate the goal in your own words.
3 Discuss the goal with a teacher or a parent.
4. Visualize the presentation and see yourself achieving the goal.

At this point the teacher needs to decide what learners—and teachers—need to know. What stories do they want to tell? What do they want their audience to know about students as learners? What outcomes would they like to result from their conferences?

For an example of goals set by students, see the Examples page at the end of this chapter. For a blackline master to help students plan this and consequent steps, see Blackline 9.3 at the end of this chapter.

Schedule Conference—On Time

The students can be involved in setting up the schedule. For student-student conferences, cooperative groups can work to create schedules for in-school presentations. When parents or others are invited for specific time-period conferences, students may contact parents to find out when they are available. In planning for whole-class or school-wide exhibitions, students can work within time allotments provided by teachers to plan the length of presentations.

Digital Connection

The planning process for a Web-based portfolio presentation parallels the traditional portfolio process. The process also parallels the teachers' consideration of the "logistics" for Web site publishing and monitoring the security of the students' telecommunication during the conferences.

Set the Date—Book It

The conference dates must be scheduled.

Design Invitations—Invites

Students need to think about how they will invite their guests to portfolio conferences. Carefully designed invitations should tell guests the purpose and theme of the conference. Students should be involved in the design of brief, informal invitations. Students can write a formal letter that includes information of what to expect and even some suggestions for conference protocol. Teachers promote learner responsibility and autonomy by encouraging students to consider these questions and to implement a plan together.

Anticipate Scheduling Problems—Conference at Home

Sometimes parents cannot attend the official portfolio conferences because of scheduling conflicts. Teachers can send home the portfolios along with guideline sheets that describe how the parents can conduct the conference at home. Sometimes teachers include sample questions to help parents start the process as well as a form for parents to record their feelings about the portfolio and the conference or give feedback on specific portfolio entries.

Determine Setup—Blueprints

Students should plan how to arrange the room or a series of the rooms needed for portfolio conferences. Students should create blueprints for display tables that will showcase artifacts from portfolios or other products and projects. They should also create posters or signs to direct guests from the entry doors to the conferences or exhibitions.

Conduct an Audience Audit—Know Your Audience

Dale Carnegie's famous book, *How to Win Friends and Influence People* (1981), advocates the idea that to reach a goal, a person must first understand others' goals or find out what the other party wants and be sure to deliver it. Students must know who their audience will be and plan to meet the expectations of this audience. Whether it's a

Audience Audit

POSSIBLE AUDIENCES	PROBABLE FOCUS
Parent(s)	Areas of progress and growth
Teacher	Evidence of required work, meeting the standards
Guidance Counselor	Areas of strengths and weaknesses
Personnel Director	Skills, quality, creativity, versatility
Peers	Quality, quantity, special artifacts that reveal personality and interests
Admissions Officer	Academic pride, talents, and skills

Figure 9.2

parent conference, a teacher evaluation, or a job interview, they need to think about what the audience will be looking for and how they can best highlight those things. The audience audit in Figure 9.2 can prepare students and teachers for the conference.

Choose Introductions—Introducing, Initiating, and Responding

If students are planning conferences for the first time, they may need some guidance in considering how they will introduce their portfolios, how they will initiate the communication with their audiences, and how they might respond to comments or questions that they may not have anticipated. By prompting student thinking about these social skills, teachers can ensure that each student will have the opportunity to practice or role-play some typical or atypical scenarios which may occur in parent-student or significant other student conferences. (For a sample introduction, see the Examples page at the end of this chapter.)

Set Protocol—Conference Etiquette

Students may establish some conference guidelines or protocol for the benefit of their audiences. Once again, the more autonomy students are given to prepare their portfolios and conference formats (within the established purposes), the more likely they will be to accept and maintain ownership of their learning processes. (For a sample protocol, see the Examples page at the end of this chapter.)

Design Questions—The Million Dollar Question

The questions asked at conferences will vary depending on the type and purpose of the portfolios and the audience. Different questions target different conference goals. Figure 9.3 provides sample questions for four types of portfolio conferences. Students and teachers should plan what questions will be asked during the conference. (See Blackline 9.4 at the end of this chapter for a sample question sheet that can be used with parents at a portfolio conference.)

Students and teachers also need to choose the nature of reflections they will use throughout the conference. What reflections do learners need to engage in? Should they prepare reflective questions or stem statements for their audience?

Honor a Time Frame—Hang the Time Frame

Everybody has experienced a presentation that drones on for too long. To avoid a boring presentation, students need to refocus. The portfolio speaks for itself in many ways, but the speaker needs to bring the overall portfolio alive. Care must be taken to target, rehearse, and actually present the portfolio within a predetermined time frame. "Hang the Time Frame" is a simple strategy to keep students on track. Students hang up a sign that gives the allotted time. Similar to a cue card, the sign reminds the student presenter to be succinct and brief. Once the time frame is hung, a peer can audit the time for a partner as they practice the presentation. Practicing with this time frame technique provides a great opportunity to hone skills and develop emphasis where desired.

> Students may establish some conference guidelines or protocol for the benefit of their audiences.

Sample Questions to Ask at Portfolio Conferences, Exhibitions, and Showcases

Goal-Setting Conference

Type: Single Learning Process (Reading)

1. How do you want to grow as a reader?
2. What strategies will you work to improve?
3. What are your goals for the next quarter?
4. How do you plan to achieve these goals?

Student-Teacher Conference

Type: Personally Satisfying Entries

1. Select one of the items in your portfolio and tell me why you selected it.
2. Do you notice a pattern in the types of entries you like the best? Explain.
3. If you would have included your least satisfying pieces, what would they be and why?
4. If you could show one entry to anyone, living or dead, who would it be?

Student-Parent-Teacher Conference

Type: Significant Achievement

1. Explain why you included some of these items.
2. In what area have you achieved the greatest improvement?
3. Why do you think you have improved so much?
4. Which one of your achievements surprises you the most? Why?
5. How have you met the standards?

Student-Student Conference

Type: Joint Work with Others

1. How do you feel about working in groups?
2. What was the biggest challenge of group work?
3. On which project or performance did your group do the best? Why?
4. If you could redo any group project, what would it be and why?
5. What social skill do you want to work on?

Figure 9.3

SkyLight Professional Development

Pick the Media—Media Event

As portfolio conferences and exhibitions continue to incorporate technology, students become creative with media. Which media will be used in the presentation? computer slide show? film? video? audiotape? Will the presentation be multimedia? If the answer to any of these options is yes, the presenter must attend to media logistics. Students need to plan the elements for their multimedia presentation, or disaster may follow. De Bono's (1992) PMI strategy may help students decide which media to include in their presentations (see Figure 9.4). By appraising the pluses (P), minuses (M), and interesting (I) aspects of a media presentation, students can have a better idea of what they may need to plan for in their media presentation.

Show Personality—What's Your Style?

Students must choose a personal style for the portfolio presentation. Personal style involves how students present themselves in public and private situations. Some students prefer a lighthearted approach, using humor to diffuse the tension that is part of any formal gathering. Others may be more comfortable presenting in a genuine, folksy way, sprinkling the presentation with personal anecdotes. Others may

PMI Chart
Using Media in a Presentation

Record the Pluses, Minues, and Interesting aspects in the chart below.

PLUS	
MINUS	
INTERESTING	

(Created by de Bono)

Figure 9.4

choose a reserved style, relying on the strength of the portfolio to carry the show. Some may select a direct approach to the presentation, dotting the monologue with pointed questions. Students should ask themselves questions about their style. One way to discover one's style is to videotape a rehearsal of the portfolio presentation for the student to analyze and reflect upon. Another way is to have students work with partners and assess each other's style through peer dialogue.

Create Openings and Closings—Gotcha

A presenter makes or breaks a presentation in the first ninety seconds. Teachers can help students see the importance of the opening and the first artifacts shown. A good close leaves the audience feeling positive. Strong openings and closings involve the same elements:

- Surprise
- Questions
- Anecdotes
- Quotes
- Questions

- Design
- Mystery Items
- Cartoons
- Graphics
- Skits

Students should choose effective openings and closings for their portfolio conferences.

Rehearse Conference Dialogue—The Rehearsal

Before the conference, it is wise to conduct a rehearsal. This will help students overcome their nervousness and offer students a chance to fine-tune their presentations. Teachers can ask students to run through their presentations in pairs or groups. While a student practices his or her presentation, another student or students act the role of the teacher, parent, or other interested audience member. Figures 9.5 and 9.6 are two sample dialogues to use as models.

Plan the Post-Conference Evaluation—So What?

As the planning for the portfolio conference comes to a close and the event approaches, it is important for students to think ahead to the "so what" of the conferences. How will they know if they were successful in meeting their goals? How do they wish to evaluate the conferences? What would they like to learn by the end of the conference? What will be valued? The teacher will want to show the students a variety of evaluation ideas including the possibility of preparing surveys or informal stem statements that request feedback from those who have had conferences with them. Students will be eager to share their experiences and to find out what their audience said about their portfolios. Both the teacher and the student participate. An example of a post-conference evaluation is on the Examples page at the end of this chapter. Also included at the end of the chapter is Blackline 9.5, which can be used as a portfolio evaluation.

In the same way that it is important to engage students in the reflection and processing of important learning experiences in the classroom, the individual student needs to self-assess the outcome of the portfolio conference, exhibition, or showcase. Whether a teacher has developed a scoring rubric for the event, or a reflection log, the conference evaluation completed by the student must be seen as an important part of the portfolio connection process. Teachers can assist students in reviewing their purposes and objectives, analyzing the data they collected from the audience evaluations, and reflecting on the comments and suggestions they received during the conferences. In addition, students can assess the social skills and habits of mind that they used during the event. This assures that each student has the opportunity to reflect on the pluses and minuses while setting goals for future portfolio exhibitions and showcases.

Sample Dialogue for a Student-Led Parent-Teacher Conference

Significant Achievement Portfolio

Student: Let me begin my portfolio conference by telling you a little bit about our portfolios and what the purpose has been since we began using them. Then I want you to look over some parts of it and ask me anything you would like.

Parent: All right. That sounds great.

Student: We use portfolios at this school because there are so many things that we are interested in learning that they all can't be shown by the tests we take.

Parent: Excuse me, you mean you don't use your tests for grades anymore.

Student: (laughing) I wish! No, you'll see tests in my portfolio that are graded. Getting back to the purpose, we agreed that our portfolios would show us and you that we are learning important things in science, math, social studies, and other things. We're learning how to solve problems, to write about things that are important to us, and to become better at working on big projects or ideas together. So our portfolios are about our achievement in all our subjects but also about who we are as people. For this conference, we decided that we would choose pieces from our whole portfolio that show significant achievement.

Parent: These are things you got your best grades on?

Student: Not always, but most of the time. Let me show you this math paper (takes a paper from folder). I selected this one and wrote my reasons here. Do you want to read it?

Parent: Yes. (Reads, then looks at math paper.) So you figured out how to do this kind of problem, even though you got many problems wrong on the quiz.

Student: Yeah. It was when we were going over our mistakes in peer study groups that I figured it out. It was a great feeling!

Parent: I'm jealous. I wish that would have happened to me in algebra.

Student: Hey, I just got what it takes! (laughs) Anyway, all the rest of the things in my portfolio are like this. They show what I've learned but they also show how and sometimes why. Let's look at some other pieces and you can ask me whatever you want to know.

The teacher participated as an observer, stopped to greet the conference attendees, listened briefly to the discussion, and urged them to continue unless they had questions.

Figure 9.5

SkyLight Professional Development

Sample Dialogue for a Teacher-Student Portfolio Conference

Personally Satisfying Portfolio

Teacher: I see you're ready to begin your portfolio conference. I'm impressed already. Your cover is great!

Student: Thanks! I got a little carried away, but I like the way it looks. It's really cool.

Teacher: Tell me about it and then let's talk about what's inside.

Student: Well, since this was our personally satisfying portfolio conference, I got to wondering. If I got an award for each best work that was one of my favorite things, what would each award be?

Teacher: I like that idea.

Student: So, I glued on the ticket stubs from the baseball game my dad took us to, and then a card of my favorite player. Here's a picture of my favorite dessert— yes, chocolate! Here's a picture from my favorite vacation. And there's a whole bunch of other stuff that I love.

Teacher: This is fun to look at. Let's see what you've put inside.

Student: (apologetic) Well, it was hard to choose work from my working portfolio that was my best, because my opinion changes.

Teacher: I'm glad you noted that. I like that you did include this writing assignment from September. It was very good.

Student: Thanks, I know it was the best. It makes me feel good to look at it now because I remember working hard on it with the computer. It's easier for me to write when I type instead of writing with a pen or pencil. It looks better when it's done.

Teacher: Don't give up on your handwriting. It gets better all the time. Can you show me a piece that you think shows work on learning an idea or about an important issue or event that was satisfying to you?

Student: (thinking) Yes. I'll show you the science presentation that I did with my group. You remember . . . .

Figure 9.6

Examples: Respect and Celebrate Accomplishments

Choose Conference Goals
PORTFOLIO CONFERENCE GOALS SET BY STUDENTS

Primary

I want my portfolio to tell my story about how I learned to read this year.

Intermediate

By the time my parents are done looking at my portfolio and talking to me about my work and the reflections I have written, I want them to be as excited as I am about how much I have improved in everything!

High School

My portfolio conference should show the teachers in this school that I have really learned how to use computers to organize and present a project on communications.

Choose Introductions
INTRODUCTIONS: WELCOME TO OUR PORTFOLIO CONFERENCE

Dear Honored Guest:

Welcome to our fifth-grade portfolio exhibition. We are pleased that you have joined us as we present the portfolios of the significant work we have achieved during the past year.

We have worked hard to select just the right pieces for our portfolios. We think they tell you the "real story" about who we are as students here at Whitman School.

The next page includes some suggestions we thought you would like to use as you visit each of our exhibits. Feel free to use any of them and to spend as much time as you like at our exhibits.

Have a good time and thank you very much for coming tonight.

Sincerely yours,
Whitman School Fifth-Grade Class

Set Protocol
PORTFOLIO CONFERENCE PROTOCOL FOR AUDIENCES

The following are some tips that the students from our school have designed to help you get the most from your portfolio conference. We hope you enjoy visiting with our students.

- Listen to the student.
- If responses are unclear, please ask for more information.
- Concentrate on one piece at a time.
- Make comments about the portfolios that can help students to look at their work from new perspectives or to value their work from another person's view.
- Ask students to tell you how they feel about their work at Washington Elementary.
- Ask if students need any help meeting standards.

Post-Conference Evaluation

Student Name: *Brian*   Grade Level: *8*
Conference Date: *11-14*

1. What were your goals?
   To share my portfolio with my parents.

2. List the goals you achieved.
   Covered all items. Answered their questions.

3. How do you feel about the conference(s)?
   Great! It's over!

4. Think of one suggestion you received during a conference that you know you want to try.
   More artwork.

5. Rate your overall portfolio conference(s).

   /————————/————————/
   Not Yet   Pretty Good   Yes! Yes! Yes!

SkyLight Professional Development

Chapter Nine

Blackline Masters

Teacher Planner
for Portfolio Conferences

Who will participate?

. . . .
. . . .
. . . .

What type of portfolio conference will be planned?

. . . .
. . . .
. . . .

What are the goals of the conference?

. . . .
. . . .
. . . .

What are the logistics?

Date: _____ Time: _____ Place: _____
Invitations: _____
_____
Room setup: _____
_____
Refreshments: _____
_____

How will you evaluate the conferences?

. . . .
. . . .
. . . .

Teacher Planner
Checklist for Exhibitions

❑ Date_____   ❑ Time_____

❑ Place

. . . .

. . . .

. . . .

. . . .

❑ Invitations

. . . .

. . . .

. . . .

. . . .

❑ Refreshments

. . . .

. . . .

. . . .

. . . .

❑ Equipment

. . . .

. . . .

. . . .

Blackline 9.2

Exhibit Your Work

Student Name:_____

Directions to Student: Think about each element and jot down your thoughts.

Scoring the Goal:

Audience Audit:

Hang the Time Frame:

Media Event:

What's Your Style?

Gotcha (Openings/Closings):

SkyLight Professional Development • www.skylightedu.com

Parent Portfolio Conference Guide

Dear Parent: Please review your son's/daughter's portfolio and ask him/her questions about his/her work. The following questions might help start the discussion. Thank you for your cooperation.

1.   What have you learned about yourself by putting together your portfolio?

2.   What is your favorite piece? Why?

3.   If you could publish one thing in this portfolio, what would it be and why?

4.   Select one item and tell how you feel about it.

Please write any comments you have and give this sheet to your son/daughter to return to school.

_____

_____

_____

_____

_____

Signed: _____ Date: _____

Blackline 9.4

Evaluation of Portfolio Conference

Student Name:_____Grade:_____

Conference Date: _____

What were your goals for this conference? _____

_____

_____

_____

List the goals you achieved. _____

_____

_____

_____

How do you feel about the conference? _____

_____

_____

_____

List at least one suggestion you received during the conference that you want
to try at the next conference. _____

_____

_____

_____

Rate your overall portfolio conference using the ratings below.

|———————|———————|———————|———————|

Not Yet   Getting Started   Pretty Good   Almost There Yes! Yes! Yes!

MY PORTFOLIO

GREEK MYTHOLOGY UNIT

**"Beware all mortals who
gaze at me alone!
Use a mirror to reflect,
or you will turn to stone!"**

Mindy "Medusa" Smith—Grade 8

GREEK MYTHOLOGY UNIT

My Portfolio
Table of Contents

LANGUAGE ARTS

"THE FIRST SUPER BOWL ON MT. OLYMPUS"

There once was a football coach named Zeus
Whose sportsmanship and morals were loose
He would lie and he'd cheat
Every team he would meet
Until Athena would call a truce.

The Greek Gods of Old Olympic High
Were conceited and quick with a lie
They'd toy with mortal men
In vain attempts to win
And on gold winged sandals they would fly.

Poseidon charged with trident in hand
Chased by the Olympus Marching Band
The next one to follow
Was Captain Apollo
Selling his newest sun lotion brand.

The mortal Greeks in the scrimmage fell
And were cast by Hades into hell
They soon began to plot
And place kicked a lot
And formed their own league—The NFL.

The Greeks took the field for the final game
To crush the Gods was the mortals' aim
The Gods endured the boo's
The Greeks wore Nike shoes
The first Super Bowl brought the Greeks fame!

—Mindy Medusa

My Best Piece!

Reflection:
I really enjoy writing poetry —especially funny poems. I try to use rhyming words that are interesting. It's hard with limericks because you have to have three words that rhyme. I'd like to write jingles for ads on television someday. I don't know what other jobs require poetry writing.

1

Standard: Students will produce writings from a variety of genres.

LANGUAGE ARTS

BIOGRAPHY OF A WORK
ITEM: LIMERICK—THE FIRST SUPER BOWL ON MT. OLYMPUS

Date	Summary
9/17	Teacher assigned a poem about Greek mythology. We could choose any type of poetry we wanted.
9/19	I started writing about the first pep rally at Olympus High using aabb rhyme scheme. Frustrating!
9/21	Didn't like the poem—It was too "sing-songy." Decided to change to limerick with aabba rhyme scheme.
9/23	Wrote *five* drafts of poems. Used ˘ / ˘ / ˘ / ˘ / ˘ / symbols to count syllables in each line to make sure I had 9-9-6-6-9 in each line. Very time consuming!
9/25	Typed poem on computer and cut out pictures to put on it. Wish I could draw better.
9/27	Read poem to the class and they thought it was Awesome! The class wants to make it into a skit to show at the exhibition.

Reflection

I think this poem is one of my best pieces. It's funny, creative, and it shows how much I know about the gods and goddesses. It also shows that I know how to write limericks—and they are not easy!

2

PHYSICAL EDUCATION

GROUP PROJECT OF OLYMPIC GAMES

Our group selected events used in the Greek Olympics and demonstrated what the events looked like. We selected the 10 meter race and discus throw and took a video of what the events looked like (video in portfolio).

Of course, I had to pretend I was a boy because girls did not participate in the early Olympics and they were not allowed to attend.

Reflection: This is not our best work. The filming of the video was difficult because we didn't use a tripod. The camera moves around too much and is sometimes out of focus. We need to learn how to edit a video. Also, our script wasn't very good. Our narrator ran out of things to say!

3

Standard: Students will integrate technology into presentations.

| LANGUAGE ARTS AND SOCIAL STUDIES |

THE MODERN-DAY LABORS OF HERCULES

Hercules was a Greek hero who was hated by Hera. Hera made Hercules go crazy and in a fit of rage he killed his wife and children. The famous 12 labors he was forced to perform were a penalty for his crimes. If Hercules were alive today, the following "Herculean tasks" could be assigned to him by Hera:

Labor 1: Make Hermes, the god of magic, reduce the U.S. deficit.

Labor 2: Bring back Elvis from the rock-and-roll underworld.

Labor 3: Reduce the Hydra-headed evils of drugs and violence in our cities.

Labor 4: Clean out the Augean sewers of New York.

Labor 5: Wrestle the god San Andreas and tie him down to prevent more earthquakes along the fault line in California.

Labor 6: Capture the winds of Aeolus in a bag to prevent hurricanes from hitting Florida.

Labor 7: Bring back the head of Madonna, the goddess whose looks turn men to stone.

Labor 8: Wrestle the evil Hulk Hogan in the land of Wrestlemania.

Labor 9: Capture the evil Harpie Sisters and cancel their syndicated talk show.

Labor 10: Fight the three-headed monster Barney who guards the entrance to "Toys R Us."

Labor 11: Harness the fire-breathing reindeer of "Santataur" from the land of the North Pole and make them bring the chariot of gifts to our school.

Labor 12: Level the plains of Woodstock and sow salt so that no music festival can "spring from the earth" again.

Reflection: I'm not too happy with this piece. At first I was going to be serious and have the modern-day Hercules conquer real problems. Then I tried to be humorous. I think I ended up somewhere in between. Should have added more artwork to this piece.

4

Standard: Students will analyze literary works.

SCIENCE

ORIGINAL MYTH TO EXPLAIN
"How We Got Lightning Bugs"

There once was a snotty Greek youth named Bugga. He was always playing practical tricks on people. He would sneak around during the night at drive-ins and flatten chariot wheels of couples who were kissing. He used to sneak up on the mortals and the gods in the dark and pull his childish pranks.

One day, however, Bugga played a trick on the wrong god. Bugga was sitting behind the stables of Mt. Olympus one night watching the nymphs prepare Apollo's horses to drive the sun chariot to bring up the sun for the new day. While no one was looking, he placed tiny walkman transistors in the horses' ears. Apollo soon arrived at the stables in all his golden splendor. The sun god radiated fire and power as he boarded his chariot, hooked up the sun to the back end, and prepared to take his daily ride to bring up the sun for the world.

When he left the stable, the horses charged ahead wildly out of control. Apollo used all his godly powers to restrain them. For you see, Bugga had inserted *heavy metal* tapes into their walkmen and the horses, crazy from the sound, were plunging toward earth and a fiery collision.

Apollo was finally able to control the fierce beasts and bring them and the sun back safely to Mt. Olympus. When he returned, he heard snickering coming from the bushes, and he uncovered Bugga laughing hysterically. Apollo realized the prank Bugga had played, and he knew he would have to punish the young punk for almost burning up the earth.

"Bugga, you think you're pretty cool, don't you?" whispered Apollo.

"What, old dude, I don't know what you're talking about," Bugga whined.

"You won't be sneaking around in the dark anymore to play your tricks. Everyone will know when you are around."

With that comment, Apollo struck Bugga with his lyre and Bugga shrunk to a small flying bug. Apollo touched the bug again, and this time Bugga's tail lit up.

"Now," laughed Apollo, "try to sneak around at night. Your glow will give you away. People will capture you in their hands and imprison you in jars. You'll be a firefly! And since you like that horrible heavy metal music so much, I'll curse you so you can never hear again!"

And to this day whenever you see a firefly—it's really Bugga. But don't try to yell to him. He can't hear you!

Reflection: I need to work on my dialogue. It doesn't sound natural yet. I also want to edit this story. I tend to be too wordy. I think I can have the same effect by "tightening up" the story. I also need to work on the ending.

5

MATH

MATH PROBLEM USING PYTHAGOREAN THEOREM

Pythagoras was a Greek mathematician who was born around 500 B.C. He later founded a school to promote the study of natural science, philosophy, and mathematics. He is most famous for discovering the relationship beween the lengths of the sides of a right triangle. I can use this theorem to find unknown lengths of a triangle.

> Pythagorean Theorem—In any right triangle with legs a and b, and hypotenuse c, $a^2 + b^2 = c^2$.

Problem: Find c, the length of the hypotenuse.

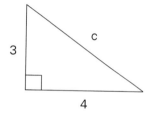

Solution:
$$a^2 + b^2 = c^2$$ Write the theorem.
$$3^2 + 4^2 = c^2$$ Substitute values for variables.
$$9 + 16 = c^2$$
$$25 = c^2$$
$$\sqrt{25} = c$$
$$5 = c$$

The hypotenuse, c, has a length of 5.

Check: $a^2 + b^2 = c^2$ substitute values
$$3^2 + 4^2 = 5^2$$
$$9 + 16 = 25$$
$$25 = 25$$

> Reflection: I'm still not too sure where I will ever use this in life. I will have to think of a word problem to write. I just know I can now verify right triangles and find missing values of right triangles.

6

ART

PRODUCTS FROM MYTHOLOGY

Ajax—Mighty Greek Warrior
and Sink Cleanser

Midas —A King with the
Golden Touch and a
Muffler

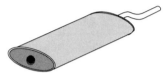

Trident—Poseidon's
Symbol and Gum

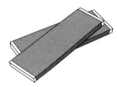

Mt. Olympus—Palace of
Gods and Olympic-sized
swimming pools

Titans—Original
Gods and Large
Ship (Titanic)

Mars—Roman God of War
and Candy Bar

Helios—Sun God and
Helium Balloons

Reflection: I have trouble drawing people, but I have learned to draw simple things in my art class. I need to take more art courses.

7

SkyLight Professional Development

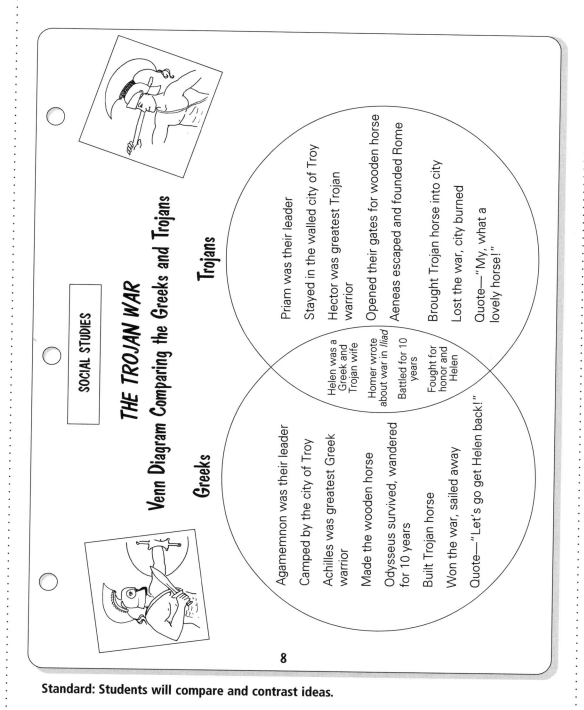

SOCIAL STUDIES

THE TROJAN WAR
Venn Diagram Comparing the Greeks and Trojans

Greeks

- Agamemnon was their leader
- Camped by the city of Troy
- Achilles was greatest Greek warrior
- Made the wooden horse
- Odysseus survived, wandered for 10 years
- Built Trojan horse
- Won the war, sailed away
- Quote—"Let's go get Helen back!"

- Helen was a Greek and Trojan wife
- Homer wrote about war in *Iliad*
- Battled for 10 years
- Fought for honor and Helen

Trojans

- Priam was their leader
- Stayed in the walled city of Troy
- Hector was greatest Trojan warrior
- Opened their gates for wooden horse
- Aeneas escaped and founded Rome
- Brought Trojan horse into city
- Lost the war, city burned
- Quote—"My, what a lovely horse!"

8

Standard: Students will compare and contrast ideas.

PORTFOLIO RUBRIC

☑ Self   ☐ Peer   ☐ Teacher

		Hades	Parthenon	Mt. Olympus
		1	2	③
1.	Creative cover	The Underworld Gazette	The Athens Chronicle	The Olympus Sun
		1	2	③
2.	Completeness	Minotaur (half man, half bull)	Perseus (half man, half god)	Zeus (all god)
		1	②	3
3.	Form (spelling, grammar, punctuation, sentence structure)	Dionysus (Sloppy—god of wine)	Odysseus (Needs help—phone home)	Hermes (Great—god of alphabet)
		1	②	3
4.	Creativity	Touched by mere mortals	Touched by the demigods	Touched by the god of creativity
		1	2	③
5.	Evidence of understanding	Hercules (Where are my Cliff Notes)	Apollo (I see the light)	Athena (Goddess of wisdom)
		1	2	③
6.	Reflection	Medusa (Never uses a mirror)	Narcissus (Gazes at own image only)	Aphrodite (Reflects in mirror on regular basis)

Comments: I know I still need to work on my sentence structure—but sometimes it gets in the way of creativity. I really don't get grammar rules. "They're Greek to me!"

Total Points: 16 = A

Scale: Total 18 pts.
15 – 18 = A
10 – 14 = B
 6 – 9 = C
Not Yet

9

SkyLight Professional Development

SELF-ASSESSMENT OF PORTFOLIO

STEM QUESTIONS

1. What is your favorite piece? Why?

My favorite piece is my limerick about the first Super Bowl on Mt. Olympus. I've always liked to write funny poems, but no one ever saw them. Now the whole class likes my poems. They've asked me to write a poem about our football team to read at the next Pep Rally. I'm really excited.

2. What piece is least satisfying to you? Why?

The group project where we videotaped some of the events from the Olympic Games. We weren't very organized and our camera work wasn't good. Sometimes it's harder to get things done right when five people have to agree. We need more team-building skills!

3. If you could share this portfolio with anyone living or dead, who would it be?

I would like to share my portfolio with my grandmother because she used to read me stories from a mythology book when I was young. I didn't like fairy tales as much as the stories of the gods and goddesses. I grew up loving Greek mythology and I'd like to share this portfolio with the person who inspired me.

10

GOAL-SETTING:

MY SHORT-TERM GOALS

Goals	Target Date
1. I need to learn how to use spell check and grammar check on my computer.	Jan. 20
2. I need to find out how to write better reflections. Mine all say about the same thing.	March 6
3. I need to find out *when* I would use the Pythagorean theorem—I don't understand why it's important.	By next test

MY LONG-TERM GOALS

Goals	Target Date
1. I want to learn how to do more computer graphics to help the layout of my portfolio and my other work.	Jan. 27
2. I want to work on my group skills. I lost my patience with group members when we did our video.	Feb. 3
3. I would like to take some elective courses in creative writing.	1996

Date of next conference: __April 3__   Signed: __Medusa Mindy__

11

ARTIFACT REGISTRY

Student _Mindy_ **Grade** _8th_ **Date** _10/5_

DELETIONS

Date	Item	Reasons
10/5	Math problem using Pythagorean Theorem	I didn't understand when and why I would need to use this.
10/5	Group project of Olympic Games Video	Poor quality. Picture moved around. Bad sound. Lots of pauses.

ADDITIONS

Date	Item	Reasons
10/5	Word problem using Pythagorean Theorem	I wrote a problem about buying fencing for my yard. Made more sense.
10/15	Group video of interviews of athletes after races	We learned how to use camera better and we wrote a good script for interviewer and athletes.

12

QUESTIONS FOR PORTFOLIO CONFERENCE

Student:_____*Mindy*_____   Date: _____*Oct. 5*_____

I have prepared the following questions that peers, parents, or teachers could ask me about my portfolio during the conference.

1. If you could become one of the mortals or gods from Greek mythology, who would you become and why?

2. If you could select one item from this portfolio to share with the whole student body, what would it be and why?

3. What subject area do you think you need to work on most? Why?

4. What do you think was the major contribution the Greeks gave the world? Explain your answer.

5. If you could board a time machine and go back to 5th century Greece for a day to interview anyone, who would it be and why?

6. Compare the fall of Troy to the fall of the Roman Empire, fall of Germany, or fall of Saigon.

7. Explain this quotation: "Beware of Greeks bearing gifts."

8. If you lived in 5th century Greece, would you rather live in Athens or Sparta? Explain why.

9. Compare the work in this portfolio to the quizzes and tests you took on Greek mythology.

10. Which item in this portfolio was the most difficult for you to do? Why?

11. What are your goals for your next portfolio?

12. Which god or goddess from mythology would be considered the most "politically incorrect" if he/she lived in the 1990s in America? Why?

13

EXHIBITION IDEAS FOR PORTFOLIO

Location: _School Gym_   **Date:** _Oct. 20_ **Time:** _10:00_

Who's Invited _Other classes, administration, parents, community members_

Description: Students and teachers dress up as their favorite character from Greek mythology. The students display their portfolios on tables as well as artifacts (posters, games, projects) they have done. Visitors are invited to talk with students and visit the four corners of the gym.

Corner #1—Refreshments – students serve ambrosia (mixed fruit), nectar (fruit juice), and grapes (food of the gods).

Corner #2—Video Corner – where copies of students' video skits and performances are shown.

Corner #3—Sports Corner – students demonstrate the athletic events that were included in the Olympic Games.

Corner #4—Music Corner – students present music of the Greeks using harps, lyres, and flutes. Groups perform Greek rap songs.

Culminating Event: Class presents original skit from mythology to group.

14

Bibliography

American Educational Research Association. 2000, November. Initial responses to AERA: Position statement concerning high-stakes testing. *Educational Researcher,* 27–30.

———. 2000, November. Position statement of the American Education Research Association concerning high-stakes testing in preK–12 education. *Educational Researcher,* 24–25.

Archbald, D. A., and F. M. Newmann. 1988. *Beyond standardized testing: Assessing authentic achievement in secondary schools.* Madison, WI: University of Wisconsin, National Association of Secondary School Principals.

Ash, L. E. 2000. *Electronic student portfolios.* Arlington Heights, IL: SkyLight Training and Publishing.

Atwell, N. 1991. *Side by side: Essays on teaching to learn.* Portsmouth, NH: Heinemann.

Barell, J. 1998. *Problem-based learning: An inquiry approach.* Arlington Heights, IL: SkyLight Training and Publishing.

Barbour, A., and B. Desjeau-Perrotta. 1998. The basics of portfolio assessment. In S.C. Wortham, A. Barbour, and B. Desjeau, eds. *Portfolio assessment: A handbook for preschool and elementary educators* (pp. 15–30). Olney MD: Association for Childhood Education Intervention.

Bass, H. 1993, October 27. Let's measure what's worth measuring. *Education Week,* 32.

Beamon, G. 2001. *Teaching with adolescent learning in mind.* Arlington Heights, IL: SkyLight Training and Publishing.

Belanoff, P., and M. Dickson. 1991. *Portfolios: Process and product.* Portsmouth, NH: Boyton & Cook Publishers.

Bellanca, J., C. Chapman, and E. Swartz. 1994. *Multiple assessments for multiple intelligences.* Palatine, IL: IRI/SkyLight Training and Publishing.

Berman, S. 1999. *Service learning for the multiple intelligences class room.* Arlington Heights, IL: SkyLight Training and Publishing.

———. 1997. *Project learning for the multiple intelligences classroom.* Arlington Heights, IL: SkyLight Training and Publishing.

Bernhardt, V. L. 1994. *The school portfolio: A comprehensive framework for school improvement.* Princeton, NJ: Eye on Education.

Board of Education of the City of New York. 1997. *New York City performance standards.* English language arts, 1st ed. New York.

Bower, B. E. 1994. *Assessment and evaluation. Mathematics in the transition years: A handbook for teachers of grade 9.* Durham, Ontario, Canada: Durham Board of Education.

Brady, G. 2000, May. The standards juggernaut. *Phi Delta Kappan,* 649–651.

Brooks, J., and M. Brooks. 1993. *In search of understanding: The case for constructivist classrooms.* Alexandria, VA: Association for Supervision and Curriculum Development.

Brown, R. 1989, April. Testing and thoughtfulness. *Educational Leadership,* 31–33.

Brown, G. and B. J. Irby. 1997. *The principal portfolio.* Thousand Oaks, CA: Corwin Press, A Sage Publication Company

Burke, C. L. 1991, August. Curriculum as inquiry. Presentation at the Whole Language Umbrella Conference, Phoenix, AZ.

Burke, K. 1999. *The mindful school: How to assess authentic learning,* 3rd ed. Arlington Heights, IL: SkyLight Training and Publishing.

———. 1997. *Designing professional portfolios for change.* (Training Manual and Book) Arlington Heights, IL: IRI/SkyLight Training and Publishing.

———, ed. 1992. *Authentic assessment: A collection.* Palatine, IL: IRI/SkyLight Training and Publishing.

Campbell, J. 1992, May. Laser disk portfolios: Total child assessment. *Educational Leadership,* 69–70.

Campbell, D., Cignetti, P. B., Melenyzer, B. J., Nettles, D. H. and Wyman, R. M. 1997. *How to develop a professional portfolio: A manual for teachers.* Needham Heights, MA: Allyn & Bacon.

Carnegie, D. 1981. *How to win friends and influence people.* New York: Simon and Schuster.

Carr, J. F., and D. E. Harris. 2001. *Succeeding with standards: Linking curriculum, assessment, and action planning.* Alexandria, VA: Association for Supervision and Curriculum Development.

Cole, D. J., C. W. Ryan, F. Kick, and B. K. Mathies. 2000. *Portfolios across the curriculum and beyond,* 2nd ed. Thousand Oaks, CA: Corwin Press, A Sage Publications Company.

Costa, A. L. 1993. Thinking: How do we know students are getting better at it? In K. A. Burke, ed. *Authentic assessment: A collection* (pp. 213–220). Palatine, IL: IRI/SkyLight Training and Publishing.

———. 1991. *The school as a home for the mind.* Palatine, IL: IRI/SkyLight Training and Publishing.

Costa, A. L., J. Bellanca, and R. Fogarty. 1992. *If minds matter: A foreword to the future, Vol. I.* Palatine, IL: IRI/SkyLight Training and Publishing.

———. 1992. *If minds matter: A foreword to the future, Vol. II.* Palatine, IL: IRI/SkyLight Training and Publishing.

Costa, A. and B. Kallick. 2000. *Habits of mind* (series of 4). Alexandria, VA: Association for Supervision and Curriculum Development.

———. 1992. Reassessing assessment. In A.L. Costa, J.A. Bellanca, and R. Fogarty, eds. *If minds matter: A foreword to the future,*

Vol. II (pp. 275–280). Palatine, IL: IRI/SkyLight Training and Publishing.

———. 1995. *Assessment in the learning organization: Shifting the paradigm.* Alexandria, VA: Association for Supervision and Curriculum Development.

Council of Chief State School Officers. 1996. Interstate School Leaders Licensure Consortium: Standards for School Leaders, Washington, D.C.

Crafton, L. 1994, April. Reflections. *Primary Voices,* 39–42.

———. 1991. *Whole language: Getting started . . . moving forward.* Katonah, NY: Richard C. Owen.

Crafton, L., and C. L. Burke. 1994, April. Inquiry-based evaluations: Teachers and students reflecting together. *Primary Voices,* 2–7.

Danielson, C. 1996. *Enhancing professional practice: A framework for teaching.* Alexandria, VA: Association for Supervision and Curriculum Development.

Darling-Hammond, L. 1997. *The right to learn: A blueprint for creating schools that work.* San Francisco: Jossey-Bass.

Darling-Hammond, L., J. Ancess, and B. Falk. 1995. *Authentic assessment in action: Studies of schools and students at work.* New York: Teachers College, Columbia University.

Davies, A., C. Cameron, C. Politano, and K. Gregory. 1992. *Together is better: Collaborative assessment, evaluation and reporting.* Winnipeg, Manitoba, Canada: Pequis Publishers.

de Bono, E. 1992. *Serious creativity.* New York: HarperCollins.

Depka, E. 2001. *Designing rubrics for mathematics: Standards, performance tasks, checklists, and student-created rubrics.* Arlington Heights, IL: SkyLight Training and Publishing.

Dichek, P., Caceres, B., and Rinaldo, S. PS146 Community School District 4, New York City.

Dietz, M. 2001. *Designing the school leader's portfolio.* Arlington Heights, IL: SkyLight Training and Publishing.

———. 1998. *Journals as frameworks for change.* Arlington Heights, IL: SkyLight Training and Publishing.

———. 1992. Professional development portfolio. In *Frameworks.* Shoreham, NY: California Professional Development Program.

Diez, M. E. 1999. Assessment in support of standards: Developing teachers' ability to use assessment well. *Assessing student learning: A practical guide.* K. Seidel, ed. CD-ROM. Alliance for Curriculum Reform.

Eisner, G. W. 1993, February. Why standards may not improve schools. *Educational Leadership,* 22–23.

Ferrara, S., and J. McTighe. 1992. Assessment: A thoughtful process. In A. L. Costa, J. Bellanca, and R. Fogarty, eds. *If minds matter: A foreword to the future, Vol. II* (pp. 337–348). Palatine, IL: IRI/SkyLight Training and Publishing.

Flavell, J. H., A. G. Fredenchs, and J. D. Hoyt. 1970. Development changes in memorization processes. *Cognitive Psychology,* 1(4): 324–340.

Fogarty, R. 2001. *Student learning standards: A blessing in disguise.* Chicago: Fogarty & Associates.

———. 1997. *Problem-based learning and other curriculum models for the multiple intelligences classroom.* Arlington Heights, IL: SkyLight Training and Publishing.

———. 1994. *The mindful school: How to teach for metacognitive reflection.* Palatine, IL: IRI/SkyLight Training and Publishing.

———. 1991. *The mindful school: How to integrate the curricula.* Palatine, IL: IRI/SkyLight Training and Publishing.

Fogarty, R., and J. Bellanca. 1989. *Patterns for thinking: Patterns for transfer.* Palatine, IL: IRI/SkyLight Training and Publishing.

Fogarty, R., and J. Stoehr. 1995. *Integrating the curricula with multiple intelligences: Teams, themes, and threads.* Palatine, IL: IRI/SkyLight Training and Publishing.

Foriska, T. J. 1998. *Restructuring around standards: A practitioner's guide to design and implementation.* Thousand Oaks, CA: Corwin Press, A Sage Publications Company.

Frazier, D., and F. Paulson. 1992, May. How portfolios motivate reluctant writers. *Educational Leadership,* 62–65.

Fusco, E., and A. Fountain. 1992. Reflective teacher, reflective learner. In A. L. Costa, J. Bellanca, and R. Fogarty, eds. *If minds matter: A foreword to the future, Vol. I* (pp. 239–255). Palatine, IL: IRI/SkyLight Training and Publishing.

Fusco, E., M. C. Quinn, and M. A. Hauck. 1993. *The portfolio assessment handbook: Writing: A practical guide for implementing and organizing portfolio evaluations.* Roslyn, NY: Berrent Publications.

Gardner, H. 1993. *Multiple intelligences: The theory in practice.* New York: HarperCollins.

———. 1983. *Frames of mind: The theory of multiple intelligences.* New York: HarperCollins.

Glasser, W. 1986. *Control theory in the classroom.* New York: Harper and Row.

Glazer, S. M. 1998. *Assessment is instruction: Reading, writing, spelling, and phonics for all learners.* Norwood, MA: Christopher-Gordon Publishers.

———. 1993, December. How do I grade without grades? *Teaching K–8,* 104–106.

Glazer, S. M., and C. S. Brown. 1993. *Portfolios and beyond: Collaborative assessment in reading and writing.* Norwood, MA: Christopher-Gordon Publishers.

Goodman, K., L. B. Bird, and Y. M. Goodman, eds. 1992. *The whole language supplement on authentic assessment: Evaluating ourselves.* New York: SRA Macmillan/McGraw-Hill.

Gratz, D. 2000, May. High standards for whom? *Phi Delta Kappan,* 681–683.

Gronlund, N. E. 1998. *Assessment of student achievement,* 6th ed. Boston: Allyn & Bacon.

Hamm, M., and D. Adams. 1991, May. Portfolio: It's not just for artists anymore. *The Science Teacher,* 18–21.

Hansen, J. 1992, May. Literacy portfolios: Helping students know themselves. *Educational Leadership*, 66–68.

Harste, J. C., V. A. Woodward, and C. L. Burke. 1984. *Language stories and literacy lessons*. Portsmouth, NH: Heinemann.

Hartnell-Young, E. and M. Morriss. 1996. *Digital professional portfolios for change*. Arlington Heights, IL: SkyLight Training and Publishing, Inc.

Hebert, E. A. 1992, May. Portfolios invite reflection—from students and staff. *Educational Leadership*, 61.

Herman, J. L., P. R. Aschbacher, and L. Winters. 1992. *A practical guide to alternative assessment*. Alexandria, VA: Association for Supervision and Curriculum Development.

Hill, B. C., and C. Ruptic. 1994. *Practical aspects of authentic assessment: Putting the pieces together*. Norwood, MA: Christopher-Gordon Publishers.

Hill, B. C., C. Ruptic, and L. Norwick. 1998. *Classroom based assessment*. Norwood, MA: Christopher-Gordon Publishers.

Hoff, R. 1992. *I can see you naked*. Kansas City, MO: Andrews and McMeel.

Illinois State Board of Education. 1997, July. *Illinois learning standards*.

Jalongo, M. R. 1992. Teachers' stories: Our ways of knowing. In K. A. Burke, ed. *Authentic assessment: A collection* (pp. 191–199). Palatine, IL: IRI/SkyLight Training and Publishing.

Jensen, E. 1995. *The learning brain*. Del Mar, CA: The Brain Store.

Jeroski, S. 1992. Finding out what we need to know. In A. L. Costa, J. Bellanca, and R. Fogarty, eds. *If minds matter: A foreword to the future, Vol. II* (pp. 281–295). Palatine, IL: IRI/SkyLight Training and Publishing.

Johnson, N. J., and L. M. Rose. 1997. *Portfolios: Clarifying, classifying, and enhancing*. Lancaster: Basil Technomic Publishing Company.

Kallick, B. 1989. *Changing schools into communities for thinking*. Grandforks, ND: University of North Dakota Press.

Kamii, C., F. B. Clark, and A. Dominick. 1994, May. The six national goals: A road to disappointment. *Phi Delta Kappan*, 672–677.

Kendall, J. S. and R. J. Marzano. 1997. *Content knowledge: A compendium of standards and benchmarks for K–12 education*, 2nd edition. Aurora, CO: Mid-Continent Regional Educational Laboratory (McREL); Alexandria, VA: Association for Supervision and Curriculum Development.

Kohn, A. 1999, May. The dark side of standards. *Education Update*, 7.

Lewin, L., and B. J. Shoemaker. 1998. *Great performances: Creating classroom-based assessment tasks*. Alexandria, VA: Association for Supervision and Curriculum Development.

Linquist, T. 1997. *Ways that work: Putting social studies standards to work*. Portsmouth, NH: Heineman.

Marzano, R.J. 2000. *Transforming classroom grading*. Alexandria, VA: Association for Supervision and Curriculum Development.

Marzano, R. J., and J. S. Kendall. 1996. *A comprehensive guide to designing standards-based districts, schools, and classrooms*. Alexandria, VA: Association for Supervision and Curriculum

Development (ASCD) and Aurora, CO: Mid-Continent Regional Educational Laboratory (McREL).

Marzano, R., D. Pickering, and J. McTighe. 1997. *Assessing student outcomes*. Alexandria, VA: Association for Supervision and Curriculum Development.

Marzano, R. J., D. J. Pickering, and J. E. Pollack. 2001. *Classroom instruction that works: Research-based strategies for increasing student achievement*. Alexandria, VA: Association for Supervision and Curriculum Development.

McDonald, J. P., S. Smith, D. Turner, M. Finney, and E. Barton. 1993. *Graduation by exhibition: Assessing genuine achievement*. Alexandria, VA: Association for Supervision and Curriculum Development.

McLaughlin, M. and M. Vogt. 1996. *Portfolios in teacher education*. Newark, DE: International Reading Association.

Midwood, D., K. O'Connor, and M. Simpson. 1993. *Assess for success: Assessment, evaluation and reporting for successful learning*. Toronto, Ontario, Canada: Educational Services Committee, Ontario Secondary School Teachers' Federation.

Mills-Courts, K., and M. R. Amiran. 1991. Metacognition and the use of portfolios. In P. Belanoff and M. Dickson, eds. *Portfolios: Process and product* (pp. 101–111). Portsmouth, NH: Baxton and Cook Publishers.

Missouri Department of Elementary and Secondary Education. 1993. *Show-me standards*. Jefferson City, MO: Missouri Department of Elementary and Secondary Education.

National Board for Professional Teaching Standards (NBPTS). 2000. *What every teacher should know*. Arlington, VA: National Board for Professional Teaching Sandards.

National Council of Teachers of Mathematics, Commission on Teaching Standards for School Mathematics. 1991. *Professional standards for teaching mathematics*. Reston, VA: National Council of Teachers of Mathematics.

Newman, F.M., A.S. Bryk, and J.K. Nagoaka. 2001, January. Authentic intellectual work and standardized tests: Conflict or coexistence? Improving Chicago Schools: Consortium on Chicago School Research. A Report of the Chicago Annenberg Research Project.

Nitko, A. J. 2001. *Educational assessment of students,* 3rd edition. Upper Saddle River, NJ: Prentice Hall.

Paulson, F. L., P. R. Paulson, and C. A. Meyer. 1991, February. What makes a portfolio a portfolio? *Educational Leadership*, 60–63.

Perna, D., and J. Davis. 2000. *Aligning standards and curriculum for classroom success*. Arlington Heights, IL: SkyLight Training and Publishing.

Popham, W. J. 2000. *Testing! Testing! What every parent should know about school tests*. Boston: Allyn & Bacon.

———. 1999. *Classroom assessment: What teachers need to know*, 2nd edition. Boston: Allyn & Bacon.

Peter, L. J. 1977. *Peter's quotations: Ideas for our time*. New York: Bantam.

SkyLight Professional Development

Ravitch, D. 1995. *National standards in American education: A citizen's guide.* Washington, D.C.: Brookings Institute.

Rolhesier, C., ed. 1996. *Self-evaluation . . . Helping students get better at it!* Ajax, Ontario, Canada: VisuTron X.

Rolheiser, C., B. Bower, and L. Stevahn. 2000. *The portfolio organizer: Succeeding with portfolios in your classroom.* Alexandria, VA: Association for Supervision and Curriculum Development.

Ross, J.A., C. Rolheiser, and A. Hogaboam-Gray. 1999. Effects of collaborative action research on the knowledge of five Canadian teacher-researchers. *The Elementary School Journal,* 99(3) 255–274.

Schmoker, M. 1996. *Results: The key to continuous school improvement.* Alexandria, VA: Association for Supervision and Curriculum Development.

Schmoker, M., and R. Marzano. 1999, March. Realizing the promise of standards-based education. *Educational Leadership,* 17.

Schmuck, R. A. 1997. *Practical action research for change.* Arlington Heights, IL: IRI/SkyLight Training and Publishing, Inc.

Shaklee, B. D., N. E. Barbour, R. Ambrose, and S. J. Hansford. (1997). *Designing and using portfolios.* Boston: Allyn & Bacon.

Silvers, P. 1994, April. Everyday signs of learning. *Primary Voices,* 20–29.

Smith, J. B., V. E. Lee, F. M. Newman. 2001, January. Instruction and achievement in Chicago elementary schools. Improving Chicago Schools: Consortium School Research. A Report of the Chicago Annenberg Research Project.

Stefonek, T. 1991. *Alternative assessment: A national perspective.* Policy Briefs No. 15 and 16. Oak Brook, IL: North Central Regional Educational Laboratory.

Stiggins, R. J. 1994. *Student-centered classroom assessment.* New York: Merrill, MacMillan College Publishing.

Tchudi, S. 1991. *Planning and assessing the curriculum in English language arts.* Alexandria, VA: Association for Supervision and Curriculum Development.

Tomlinson, C. A. 1999. *The differentiated classroom: Responding to the needs of all learners.* Alexandria, VA: Association for Supervision and Curriculum Development.

Tomlinson, C. A., and S. D. Allan. 2000. *Leadership for differentiating schools and classrooms.* Alexandria, VA: Association for Supervision and Curriculum Development.

Vavrus, L. 1990, August. Put portfolios to the test. *Instructor,* 48–53.

Visovatti, K. 1994, April. Developing primary voices. *Primary Voices,* 8–19.

Wiggins, G. 1994. *Standards, not standardization* [Videotape]. Distributed by Sunburst/Wings for Learning, 101 Castleton Street, P.O. Box 100, Pleasantville, NY 10570-0110.

———. 1993. *Assessing student performance: Exploring the purpose and limits of testing.* San Francisco: Jossey-Bass.

Wiggins, G., and J. McTighe. 1998. *Understanding by design.* Alexandria, VA: Association for Supervision and Curriculum Development.

Wolf, D. 1989, April. Portfolio assessment: Sampling student work. *Educational Leadership*, 35–39.

Worthen, B. 1993, February. Critical issues that will determine the future of alternative assessment. *Phi Delta Kappan*, 444–456.

Wortham, S. C. 2001. *Assessment in early childhood education*, 3rd ed. Upper Saddle River, NJ: Merrill Prentice Hall.

Zemelman, S., H. Daniels, and A. Hyde. 1998. *Best practice: New standards for teaching and learning in American schools.* Portsmouth, NH: Heineman.

Zimmerman, J., (Ed.). 1993, November. Student portfolios: Classroom uses. *Research Education Consumer Guide*, 8, 1.

Index

SkyLight Professional Development

**CORWIN
PRESS**

The Corwin Press logo—a raven striding across an open book—represents the union of courage and learning. Corwin Press is committed to improving education for all learners by publishing books and other professional development resources for those serving the field of K–12 education. By providing practical, hands-on materials, Corwin Press continues to carry out the promise of its motto: **"Helping Educators Do Their Work Better."**